THE 1-2-2 OFFENSE FOR WINNING BASKETBALL

THE 1-2-2 OFFENSE
FOR WINNING BASKETBALL

Carroll Smith

PARKER PUBLISHING COMPANY, INC.
WEST NYACK, NEW YORK

©1976 *by*

Parker Publishing Company, Inc.
West Nyack, New York

Library of Congress Cataloging in Publication Data

Smith, Carroll,
    The 1-2-2 offense for winning basketball.

    Includes index.
    1. Basketball--Offense.   I. Title.
GV889.S55   796.32'32   75-26544
ISBN 0-13-635284-7

Printed in the United States of America

Introduction

The 1-2-2 Offense for Winning Basketball was written specifically to give coaches an in-depth look at the 1-2-2 offensive alignment and to show how to incorporate the offense to meet each coach's needs. Regardless of the style of basketball a coach is currently using, this book will supply new and exciting options to improve your team's offensive scoring punch. All patterns and special plays have been proved in competition to be successful and will help each coach get the maximum results from the material on hand.

For the coach with experienced personnel and good talent, the Basic 1-2-2 Offense presented in Chapter 1 is highly recommended. This basic offense allows for sound individual initiative on offense, or may easily be adapted to a more patterned approach. The Basic 1-2-2 may be used quite successfully against all kinds of defenses and is very difficult to scout.

Strictly regimented set plays are described in detail in the chapters on the Clearout Series, the Exchange Series, the Stack Series and the Scramble Series. The Clearout Series is well suited for the team with an outstanding offensive point man. The Exchange Series and the Scramble Series are designed for the teams with or without big men and involve a lot of player movement to counter the opponent's size advantage. Both series may be used to conceal another offensive attack. Chapter 8 tells how this may be accomplished.

The Red Cat Shuffle and the Wheel show exciting continuity or shuffle patterns. These two patterns with their countless options present opportunities to score quickly or to slow down the tempo completely until a lay-up is obtained.

How to select the offensive series to fit your personnel is clearly described in Chapter 6 on Special Play Offense. This series combines the Basic 1-2-2 Offense with special plays designed for specific types of players. Explanations are given on how to evaluate returning personnel and how to fit individual talents into a winning offensive system.

Offensive basketball from baseline to baseline is stressed in the chapter entitled "Auxiliary Offense to Supplement the 1-2-2." Quick scoring out-of-bounds and jump-ball plays, plus an out-of-bounds play for every defense, are presented. Three successful methods of attacking full-court presses are described and fully illustrated.

The Blitz and Rotate Series against zone defenses is another dynamic feature of the book. Drive the opponents out of zone defenses with this quick-hitting zone attack.

To facilitate the teaching of the various offensive series described in the book, important drills are included. Develop good ball handlers through these special drills. Chapter 11 shows the offensive drills that are the very heart of making each pattern work.

The 1-2-2 Offense for Winning Basketball goes one step beyond most books on offensive basketball by giving specific details that make each pattern work. I hope each coach will find many new wrinkles that will help win the big championship.

Carroll Smith

CONTENTS

7

CHAPTER 1

Installing the
1-2-2 Offensive System

The selection of an offensive system that provides a wide variety of options to fit the personnel on hand is one of the most critical decisions a basketball coach must make. There are literally dozens of offenses from which a coach may choose. Thus, selecting an offensive system presents many problems for the coach. The offensive options presented in this book have been used successfully during the past 15 years with a wide variety of player personnel.

At the first coaching clinic I ever attended as a basketball coach, I was fortunate to hear Adolph Rupp, the great former basketball coach at the University of Kentucky, as the featured speaker. One quote really stuck in my mind and has been instrumental in the accumulation of the material for this book. Coach Rupp said, "Select an offensive system early in your career and then learn all you can about it. Don't change from system to system just because some high-pressure salesman coach has had success with an offense. However, listen to and use the things that may fit into your system." This advice has stuck with me throughout my coaching career.

The offensive system I selected was the 1-2-2 offense. From the day I first heard Coach Rupp, I have been studying and accumulating information about the 1-2-2 system. *The 1-2-2 Offense for Winning Basketball* is an accumulation of the offensive patterns that have been tested and proven successful for me.

One additional thought should be interjected at this point. I am firmly convinced that a coach can win with any type of offensive alignment. The secret or key to all successful offenses is the way the players *execute* the offense.

REASONS FOR SELECTING THE 1-2-2 OFFENSIVE ALIGNMENT

There are several reasons I decided to use the 1-2-2 alignment over the 2-1-2 or 1-3-1 formations. Some of the most important reasons are:

More Flexibility in Using Existing Personnel

This reason is especially true on the high school and junior high levels where most coaches must play with whatever material tries out for the team. Colleges may recruit a specific type of player for each position, thus making it easier to maintain a relatively consistent type of personnel.

Generally, there are three basic types of team combinations from which the coach has to choose:

1. Three quick guards and two big men;
2. Four big men and one quick guard; or
3. Two quick guards, two forwards and one big man.

These combinations can easily be fitted into the 1-2-2 offensive alignment effectively. Other combinations are also possible, but these are the most prevalent groups.

Specialization of Coaching Assignments

Most coaching staffs, even on the college level, are composed of two coaches or less for the varsity squad. Also, many assistant coaches must work as assistant football coaches on the high school level, thus making it necessary for the varsity coach to organize his practice sessions very carefully in order to teach all of the required skills properly. In the majority of cases, there is only one coach to do everything. So, by specializing his coaching assignments, a coach can break his squad into two groups in the 1-2-2 alignment, as opposed to three groups in the standard 2-1-2 alignment. Group one is composed of all of the guards, while group two is made up of all of the post men. Fundamental drills may then be grouped into these two categories.

The coach may work with group one while group two works on assigned shooting drills. Then, while the coach works with group two, group one goes through the assigned shooting drills. I have also used one of our student managers to time drills (such as rope jumping and agility drills) while I work with one group.

If an assistant coach is available, he takes one group while I take the other. We will work from 45 minutes to 60 minutes daily in our groups before coming together for team drills. We have found this to be a major advantage of the 1-2-2 system.

More Advantages for One Guard Out Front

The one-guard offense allows the point man more room to operate out front. It is more difficult to double-team since the defensive wing guard must travel a longer distance than in the 2-1-2 formation.

Another major advantage is that it is much easier to find one good ball-handling guard than two. Every squad usually has one superior guard. Thus, he becomes our point man. To me, this is the most important position on the team. The point man should be an extension of the coach. He must relay the coach's instructions to the team. Without a good offensive playmaker, few teams are successful.

Still another advantage of the one-guard front offense is that there are four possible entry points to begin the offense as opposed to three in the 2-1-2 and 1-3-1 alignments. This fact helps take the pressure off the point man.

Many coaches are reluctant to use a one-guard front offense if they do not have a good, quick, outstanding player for the point position. I firmly believe a coach can teach a boy to use a variety of offensive moves to advance the ball any place on the court, even if the opponent's defensive man is much quicker. We teach a wide variety of one-on-one maneuvers and practice them daily under pressure. More will be written about this phase of developing the point man later in this book.

Most defensive books and articles are written showing drills and defenses against the 2-1-2 alignment rather than against the 1-2-2 alignment

At most clinics, and in most books and magazine articles, defensive drills are designed and described for stopping the 2-1-2 alignment since it is the most widely used formation. This was another reason I decided to use the 1-2-2 alignment. Opponents must make special adjustments against the 1-2-2 that may vary from the standard drills.

Better Offensive Rebounding Possibilities

I feel the rebounding assignments are easier to teach from this formation. Post men are always assigned to cover each side of the basket with the off-side wing guard crashing the middle. Many times we will send both post men and both wing guards to the offensive board. The distance our post men have to travel to the ball is shorter, thus allowing us to get to the ball more quickly. I realize the opponents are also closer, but the 1-2-2 formation will often force our opponents who use the 2-1-2 formation to assign a forward to cover one of our post men. This assignment may be strange to the opponent, which will be an advantage for our post man. Also, the other opponent's forward must cover one of our wing guards. This may be more difficult for him if he has not very often played defense from the wing guard position. We feel these advantages far outweigh the disadvantages in our planned rebounding attack.

To Be Different

This may seem like a strange reason for selecting an offensive alignment, but when I moved to the East Tennessee area, the vast majority of the teams were using the 2-1-2 offensive alignment. I felt the 1-2-2, being different, would create some unique problems for the opposing coaches. They would have to work on our offense in a slightly different manner and this could have a confusing effect on the players on the other teams.

We also incorporated the match-up, and the run-and-jump defenses, before most teams in our area. This "being different" concept will not be successful unless a coach really works to sell his ideas to his players. Believing in what you are doing and conveying these beliefs to the players are the real secrets of success in coaching.

To counteract my reasons for being different (forcing our opposing coaches to change their practice sessions just to prepare for us), it should be noted that we incorporate some of the most frequently used 2-1-2 plays in our offensive repertoire so our staff will not encounter the same type of coaching problems we are trying to create for our opponents.

We use the Shuffle and Wheel offenses to teach ball handling. One season, when we had basically four guards in our line up, we went exclusively to the Wheel offense from a two-guard front because the team ran the drills so well. The team won 23 games and lost only one during the regular season. No player was over 6′ 3″. These two offensive series can be run separately or mixed with other 1-2-2 series. (For further details, see Chapter 5, "The Red Cat Shuffle," and Chapter 7, "The Wheel.")

Also included in our offensive and defensive preparations will be basic offensive plays and special defenses used by traditional opponents. This aids in preparing to meet these teams successfully each season.

ALIGNMENT OF PERSONNEL IN THE 1-2-2 ALIGNMENT
AND PLAYER REQUIREMENTS FOR EACH POSITION

Assigning players to the positions at which their individual abilities will be best used is an essential part of developing a successful team offense. A coach must know each player's strengths and weaknesses and provide his players with an offense that will use the strengths and minimize the weaknesses. Many coaches put in beautiful offensive plays and teach their players how to run them, but in the end the players often do not have the necessary offensive skills to make the offense successful. Teach the skills necessary to the players and fit the offense to their abilities.

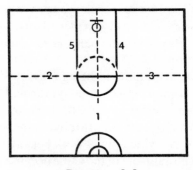

Diagram 1-1.

The alignment of each player in a specific spot is done to give the point man a starting position for each player. He knows where each man is each time we run the offense and can adjust and move the players by his signal or by a predetermined call by the coach.

The Point Man

The point man, or No. 1 man, should initiate the offense from the top of the circle or within two strides from that area. He should be in line between the basket and the mid-court circle. The reason we want the ball at this point is so the offense may be initiated to either wing guard or post man. This also helps eliminate defensive support from the opponent's wing guards. (See Diagram 1-1.)

To teach the point man to bring the ball to the desired position, we drill daily in preseason practice on the following maneuvers off the dribble:

1. The Stop-and-Go.
2. The Stutter.
3. The Crossover.
4. The Whirl or Reverse.
5. Between the Legs Change of Direction.
6. Behind the Back Change of Direction.
7. Combining Moves.

Each guard is taught these offensive dribble maneuvers and how to use them to get to the desired spot on the court. We use constant pressure, man-to-man defense and drill daily on these drills. Stress the importance of developing the ability to get the ball where you want it to initiate the offense.

The point man, in addition to being a good ball handler, must be taught all offensive combinations in our system and be able to recognize the opponent's defenses and what is the best way to attack them from our offensive system. We give each guard a mimeographed index of plays and include a chart showing which plays work best against which defense. The point man must be a student of the game because he is an extension of the coaching staff on the floor. He should be a good leader and be highly respected by the other players. He is the offensive quarterback and our success as a team is highly dependent on his success.

On our varsity squad we train three point men. (The number three point man can also play wing guard.) By doing this we are always covered in case of injury or illness to a player at this critical spot.

The Wing Guards

During the past 15 years, we have had three types of wing guards. The first type is two quick guards, usually in the 5′9″ to 6′1″ range. The second type is two tall forwards who are not extremely quick at these spots. The third type is a combination of these first two, one quick guard and one forward.

The University of Tennessee offense, under Coach Ray Mears, uses the third type. The right wing guard is always the second guard and many times the best offensive one-on-one player. The other wing guard is usually 6′5″ to 6′7″ and is good rebounder and offensive forward.

A coach can fit his personnel in almost any combination with the 1-2-2 alignment. These combinations cannot fit the 2-1-2 alignment as well.

The wing guards should be excellent outside shooters. To develop shooters, we have assigned spot shooting daily. Each man is given a specific shooting program and he must work on this program each day. This is an area where many coaches fail. They expect a player to shoot during the period prior to organized team drills, but do not give the players specific assignments that are a part of the offense from which to work.

Many of my players have gone to various levels of college basketball and 90 percent of them, when discussing their college practices, indicate that they spend very little time in organized shooting. It is my belief that a coach should constantly stress shooting and make sure each player has a designated shooting program which he follows. This is insurance which will give results at the end of a properly executed offensive pattern.

The wing guards should be included in rebounding drills daily. They are also taught to be able to bring the ball down court under tough defensive pressure. This is stressed in our group work which is done daily.

The wing guards must move without the ball. This is done in order to get open for the entry passes and to cut behind various types of screens.

We want the wing guard to receive the ball no higher than the free-throw line extended. This allows him to be in a good position to shoot a high-percentage shot or make a good short pass to one of his teammates or to be in a position to drive the basket. We teach the guard to get the ball on the shoulder away from his defensive man and immediately pivot to face the basket. He can then be in a position to shoot, pass or dribble. Under no circumstances do we want him to turn his back on the basket and away from the other four teammates.

The Post Men

The post men line up in a position just above the rectangle on each side of the free-throw lane. The main reason we stress setting up at this particular point is that they will still have enough room to operate offensively with a drop step to either the baseline or to the inside equally well and still be able to shoot the basketball. Both spots are interchangeable in our Wildcat Rotation. In the Tennessee Rotation, the number four man is usually the most mobile offensive threat, while the number five man is a big, slow rebounder.

Both men should be good rebounders at both ends of the floor. In group drills we teach jumping and rebounding drills daily, along with the offensive post maneuvers such as the drop step, hook shots to both the inside and outside, jump shots to the inside and outside and various fake and drive moves, in order to make each post man a definite offensive threat.

Both post men are taught legal screening and roll techniques and proper passing techniques. This offense provides many options to use the offensive talents of a big post man. Establishing a good inside attack is essential to playing winning basketball at any level. Later, we will discuss how a coach can have an effective inside game with short post men.

THE BASIC 1-2-2 OFFENSE

The Basic 1-2-2 Offense is initiated by a pass to either wing guard. All plays run to one side may be mirrored on the other side, so most plays will be diagrammed to only one side of the court.

Wing Guard Entry to Basic Rotation. Point man 1 passes to wing guard 3. 4 cuts to a high post position just outside the free-throw line extended and sets a screen for 1. 1 fakes left and cuts right, trying to brush

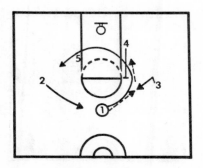

Diagram 1-2.

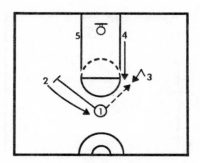

Diagram 1-3.

off his man on the screen being set by 4. 3 may pass to cutter 1 if he is open (Diagram 1-2).

"Pass-Go Away". An alternate cut by 1 may be preferred if the coach wants to keep 1 out of the play after his entry pass is made. 1 passes to 3 and goes away from the ball to screen for the offside-wing guard. We have used this option at times when 1's defensive man sags in the lane to help against our post options (Diagram 1-3).

After the initial entry pass is made, the following options are available for the wing guard:

1. To shoot the set or jump shot;
2. To drive the baseline and shoot; and
3. To drive the middle and shoot (Diagram 1-4).

In the event of heavy pressure on the wing guard on the entry pass, 3 can drive quickly to the basket and shoot either the lay-up or jump shot (Diagram 1-4).

3 may also pass to 4 and cut to the basket or to the baseline. The quick give-and-go play can provide several quick baskets, especially when the offensive wing guard is quicker than the defensive wing guard. A fake to the middle and a cut to the basket is also effective (Diagram 1-5).

3 may also pass to 4 and cut to the middle after faking a baseline cut. He may receive a pass from 4 and run the pick-and-roll play with 4 if a defensive switch occurs (Diagram 1-6). Because of the angle from which the play is being executed, there is very little defensive help since all

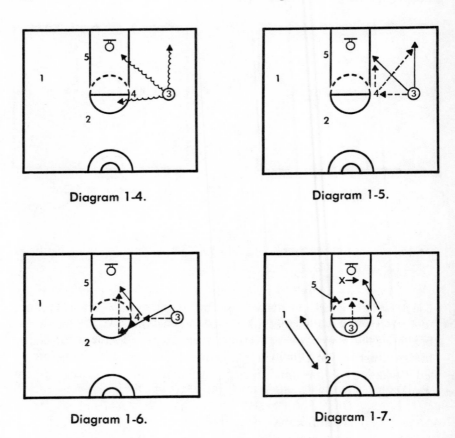

Diagram 1-4.   Diagram 1-5.

Diagram 1-6.   Diagram 1-7.

offensive men are now only one pass away from the ball and each defensive man must worry about his own man. If 5's man switches to help on 4, 3 may pass to 5 who steps toward the ball. He can shoot the jump shot or hook shot (See Diagram 1-7).

On this variation we have 2 and 1 exchange positions to further eliminate the defensive help. Also, 1 can get the ball back from 3 if we have not obtained a shot (Diagram 1-7).

If 3 passes the ball to 4 and cuts to the middle and does not get the return pass, 3 continues on over to screen for 2 who cuts around screen by 3 and receives ball from 4. 2 may shoot the jump shot immediately after receiving the ball, drive the baseline and shoot whenever open, or run the pick-and-roll option with 4 (Diagram 1-8).

A special pick and roll option may be initiated by 3. He calls the name

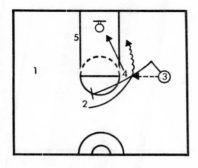

Diagram 1-8.   Diagram 1-9.

of the post man 4. This keys a screen by 4 on 3's defensive man. 3 may drive the middle and shoot or pass to 4 who rolls out to the basket (Diagram 1-9).

Caution: Teach the legal method of screening. In our area, the offensive block is called often. The screen and roll is a very vulnerable play to this call, so we over-emphasize the proper way to screen and roll. A second hint is to make the man who rolls out be aware of running into a helping defensive man.

We teach our post men always to roll out facing the basketball so they never lose sight of it. The next step is to add four additional verbal signals to get the post men free on the inside.

3, after using any of the previously diagrammed options, calls "Roll." 4 immediately turns and moves across and down the lane area to set a screen on 5's defensive man. 5 should take one step, fake toward the basket and cut to the ball around the screen. 5 may shoot or pass to 3 who cuts to the middle after faking toward the baseline or cuts to the basket after step-faking to the middle (Diagram 1-10). This option adds additional movement which is essential on any offensive formation.

The second call that may be made by 3 is the "Fan" option. 3 calls out "Fan." 4 slides down the side of the lane and across to the weak side. At the same time, 5 cuts hard to the ball to receive a pass from 3 (Diagram 1-11). 3 may pass and cut or call the name option as in Diagram 1-9.

The third call by 3 is the "Away" option. 3 calls "Away." 4 moves across the lane and down to replace 5 who fakes the Fan cut and cuts behind his defensive man to establish a low post position to receive a possible pass from 3 (Diagram 1-12).

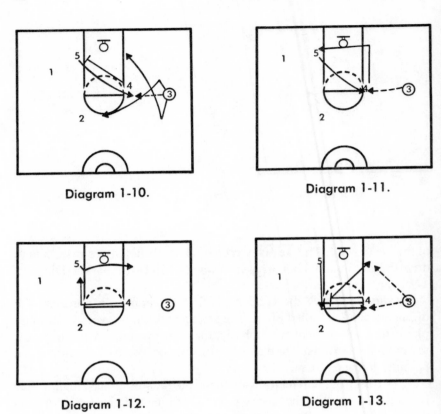

Diagram 1-10.   Diagram 1-11.

Diagram 1-12.   Diagram 1-13.

The fourth option is to call "Twist." After 3 makes this call, 5 moves to a high post position opposite the ball. 4 then screens 5's defensive man, twists and rolls back to the basket low. 5 cuts hard off 4's screen to the ball. He may receive a pass from 3, who passes and cuts as before (Diagram 1-13).

To add variety, we can insert the guard outside option. 1 passes to 3 and cuts outside of 3 to get a return hand-off. 3 then cuts off of a screen set by 4 and down to the basket where he may receive a return pass from 1. If he does not receive the ball, he cuts on through to the spot originally occupied after 1 made the first cut (Diagram 1-14). At this point, 1 becomes a wing guard and may run any of the previously described options available for the wing guards.

Diagram 1-15 shows how to add a quick counter play for more

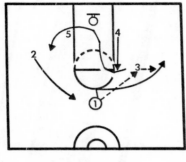

Diagram 14.

Diagram 1-15.

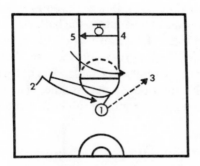

Diagram 1-16.

continuity with all of the same options available as before. 1 passes to 3 and cuts through. 3, instead of using the basic options, passes back out front to 2, the left wing guard, who rotated to the point position when 1 cut through. 2 dribbles over and passes to 1 who has cut through and becomes the 2 or left wing guard. After passing to 1, 2 cuts through around a screen set by 5. 4 drops down low and 3 rotates out to become the safety man.

The most recent innovation was added when we found ourselves with two post men who measured 6′ 3″ and 6′ 1″. Both these men had above average jumping ability and were our best rebounders, despite the lack of height. Instead of having the post man on the ball side come up high and screen, we added an automatic post rotation each time an entry pass went from the point man to a wing guard. Diagram 1-16 shows the automatic post rotation that we call our "Wildcat Rotation".

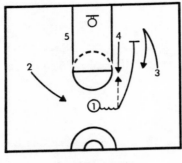 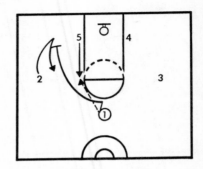

Diagram 1-17.   Diagram 1-18.

"Wildcat Rotation". As soon as the entry pass goes from 1 to 3, 5 fakes one step to the basket and cuts to the ball. At the same time, 4 cuts across the lane to replace 5 (Diagram 1-16). This simple cut gives us more movement and makes it easier to pass into the lane. 3 has all the wing guard options available once the rotation is made. Any of the four post calls may be used to vary the rotation in the middle. These cuts present the opponents' defense with even more problems to adjust to than with the basic patterns.

Options with Entry Pass to Post Men

In the event of unusually tough defensive pressure on our wing guards, we insert a rule which states that anytime we are having difficulty making the entry pass to either wing guard, the post man on the ball side will come up.

The point man now has an additional entry point to initiate the offense. We call these post entry passes the automatics. Diagram 1-17 shows an entry pass to post man 4.

The point man calls "Up" and the post man cuts up to the high-side post position just outside the lane. 1 can now pass to 4 to begin an offensive play. As soon as 1 makes the entry pass to 4, 3 reverse-cuts to the basket. In the meantime, 1 goes down and sets a screen for 3, who cuts back toward the ball for a pass from 4. 4, after receiving the ball, pivots to face the basket. He can now see 3 and 1 (Diagram 1-17).

Diagram 1-18 shows the same play to the left side. 1 calls "Up." 5 cuts up to the high-side post position to receive a pass from 1. 2

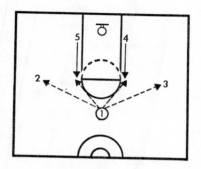

Diagram 1-19.

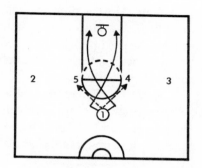

Diagram 1-20.

reverse-cuts to the basket and cuts back to the ball behind a screen set by 1 (Diagram 1-18).

A variation is sometimes added by having both post men cut up to the high-side post positions as the ball is moved to the head of the circle (Diagram 1-19). This option creates a 1-4 alignment and poses additional problems for teams employing off-side help. Four entry passes are now available for the point men and the automatics may be run to either side.

In addition to the automatic plays on the post entries, we have effectively used a quick give-and-go pattern (Diagram 1-20). With both post men in the "Up" position, 1 may pass to either 4 or 5. After making the pass to either post man, 1 fakes one step to the ball and immediately cuts to the basket. This simple give-and-go pattern has produced several easy baskets, especially in the late stages of a game when 1 has been cutting on the outside of the post men. A quick point man or one who fakes well without the ball can use this option whenever he feels he can beat his man. The ball-side wing guard rotates out front to become the defensive safety man.

OFFENSIVE REBOUNDING AND DEFENSIVE
SAFETY ASSIGNMENTS

All successful offensive teams have two common characteristics. They shoot a high percentage of field goal attempts and they secure a high percentage of second or third shots through outstanding offensive rebounding. Most winning teams combine these two characteristics.

In the 1-2-2 offensive system described in this book, heavy emphasis will be given to offensive rebounding, and assigned offensive rebounding positions with accompanying defensive safety assignments will be diagrammed in depth.

Note: On all diagrams showing offensive rebounding and defensive safety assignments reference will be made back to the offensive diagrams shown previously in the chapter. This feature will assist the coach in teaching this important phase of the game.

Identification of Rebounding and Safety Positions

Diagram 1-21 shows the various positions we hope to establish in our offensive rebounding and defensive safety plans. The side of the court on which the ball is shot is referred to as the ball side of the court. The side of the court away from the ball is referred to as weak side or off side. The position in front of the basket is referred to as the front position. The area at the free-throw line, also in front of the basket, is the combination defensive safety support position and the outlet pass delay position. There are three outside defensive safety positions shown in Diagram 1-21. S1 is between the top of the circle and the mid-court circle, S2 is on the left side of the basket, and S3 is on the right side of the basket. Both positions are about midway between the top of the circle and the mid-court circle.

Methods of Theories of Offensive Rebounding

We use two basic methods or theories of offensive rebounding. In the first method, we send four men to the basket and assign one man as the defensive safety man. In method two, we send three men to the basket and assign two men as the defensive safety men.

These two methods may be adjusted to suit a particular game plan. For example, we may be using the Follow 3-Safety 2 method, but assign one of the two safety men to go to a specific outlet pass area. The other safety man must not let a pass go behind him at any time.

A second variation of the Follow 3-Safety 2 method is to let the safety man assigned to position S2 cover the outlet pass on the left side while the man assigned to S3 covers the outlet pass on the right side of the court. Scouting will assist the coach in preparing his offensive rebounding and defensive safety assignments. Detailed preparation in this vitally neg-

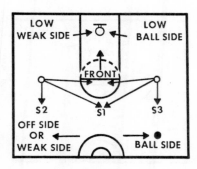

Diagram 1-21.

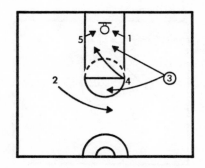

Diagram 1-22.
(See Offensive Diagram 1-2.)

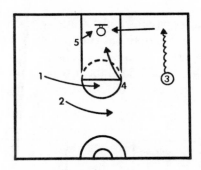

Diagram 1-23.
(See Offensive Diagrams 1-3, 1-4 and 1-5.)

lected area can provide the coach with many additional baskets while cutting down on most of the opponents' cheap baskets.

The following diagrams will further illustrate the offensive rebounding and defensive safety assignments for the basic 1-2-2 offense described in this chapter.

On a shot by 1, the following rebound assignments are to be made: 5 fills the off-side low position; 1 fills the low ball-side position; 4 fills the front spot; 3 fills the optional rebounding and outlet safety positions with 2 the defensive safety (Diagram 1-22).

5 fills the off-side low spot; 3 fills the ball-side low spot; 4 fills the front spot with 1 going to the optional spot and 2 moving to the defensive safety position (Diagram 1-23).

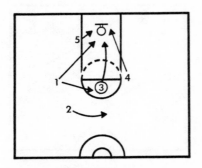

Diagram 1-24.
(See Offensive Diagrams 1-6 or 1-7.)

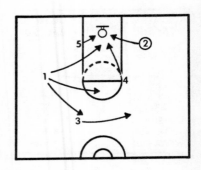

Diagram 1-25.
(See Offensive Diagram 1-8.)

On shot by 3 after passing and cutting by 4, 4 and 5 fill the two low positions; 1 moves to the optional position with 2 dropping out to the defensive safety position (Diagram 1-24).

With 2 shooting, 2 and 5 fill the low positions, 4 cuts to the front position while 3 becomes the defensive safety man (Diagram 1-25).

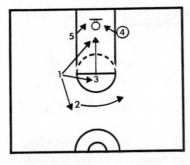

Diagram 1-26.
(See Offensive Diagram 1-9.)

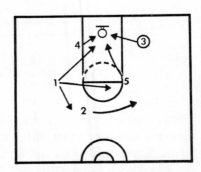

Diagram 1-27.
(See Offensive Diagram 1-10.)

Diagram 1-26 shows the assignments if 4 shoots the ball. 4 and 5 fill the two low areas. 3 fills the front position. 1 fills the optional spot and 2 becomes the defensive safety man.

In Diagram 1-27, 3 takes the shot. 3 and 4 rebound in the low

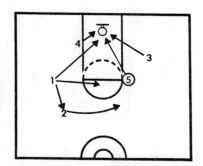

Diagram 1-28.
(See Offensive Diagram 1-11.)

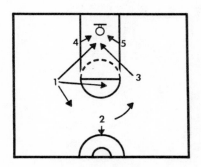

Diagram 1-29.
(See Offensive Diagram 1-12.)

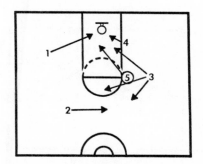

Diagram 1-30.
(See Offensive Diagram 1-13.)

spots, 5 fills the front position, with 1 taking the optional spot and 2 becomes the defensive safety man.
the safety man.

5 shoots. 3 and 4 fill the low spots. 5 rebounds the front position. 1 moves to the optional assignment and 2 moves out to become the defensive safety man (Diagram 1-28).

5 shoots on the away pattern. 4 and 5 fill the low spots. 3 rebounds the front area. 1 moves to the optional spot as 2 rotates out to the defensive safety area (Diagram 1-29).

In Diagram 1-30, 5 shoots from the high post area. 1 and 4, being the closest to the low rebounding spots, fill quickly. 5 rebounds the front area. 3 fills the optional area as 2 rotates to the defensive safety spot.

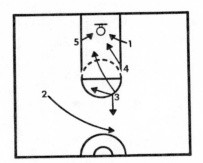

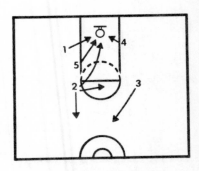

Diagram 1-31.
(See Offensive Diagram 1-17.)

Diagram 1-32.
(See Offensive Diagram 1-18.)

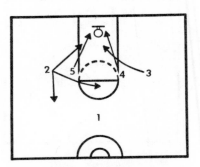

Diagram 1-33.
(See Offensive Diagrams 1-19 or 1-20.)

3 shoots in Diagram 1-31. 5 and 1 rebound low, 4 rebounds the front spot. 3 cuts to the basket or to the optional spot. 2 becomes the safety man.

In Diagram 1-32, 2 shoots. 1 and 4 fill the low positions. 5 rebounds the front area. 2 rebounds or goes to the optional area. 3 rotates out to become the defensive safety man.

On a shot by 5, 4 and 5 rebound low, 3 the front, 2 the optional area, and 1 remains out front for the defensive safety spot (Diagram 1-33).

Some coaches teach the shooter always to follow his shot. We subscribe to this theory most of the time, even though we obtain very few shots by the shooter on shots taken beyond the 15-foot range and from the sides. There have been times when we tell our outside shooters to rotate out to help on the defensive safety positions rather than follow their shots. Each coach must decide what is best for his particular team in regard to this assignment.

The 1-2-2 offense shown in this chapter may be used as the entire offensive system against man-to-man defenses or it may be used as the base offense from which to build a more complex offensive system. When we first began using the 1-2-2 alignment, we installed the basic plays in this chapter with our freshman and junior varsity teams. Each year we would add to the basic offense, including offensive series or specific plays that fit the specific talents of the current varsity squad. We have found this to be a highly desirable method of building a complete well-rounded offense over the years.

CHAPTER 2

Developing the Clearout Series
for the 1-2-2 Offense

This series emphasizes:

1. Two-on-Two Basketball.
2. Pick-and-Roll Plays.
3. Swing-and-Go Plays.
4. One-on-One Isolation.

In our section of the country, The University of Tennessee has had a considerable impact on high school basketball during the era of Coach Ray Mears. The basic philosophy of the Tennessee offense is to get the basketball to the best shooters and give them room to operate, either one-on-one or two-on-two. Players are placed in the offensive alignment according to their special skills. The best one-on-one player is usually at the right-wing guard spot. The point man gives him the ball and clears out to allow him to work one-on-one or two-on-two using the post man as a screener. This system has proven successful for the Volunteers.

When we developed the Clearout Series, we utilized many of the same principles described above. However, we wanted to develop these ideas to be used with an outstanding point man. Thus, we changed the angle of attack from the wing to the point and developed a series of two-man plays we called the "Clearout Series." To counter sagging, supporting off-side defensive men, we added the Swing Option to be used with all four of the basic Clearout Options.

THE REGULAR CLEAR OPTION

Our initial option was the Regular Clear Option and was keyed by the point man 1 simply calling "clear." On hearing the call, wing guard 3 takes a jab step toward the point man with his left foot and reverses to the basket quickly. If 3 beats his man, the point man hits him with a quick pass. If 3 does not receive a pass from 1, he sets up on the opposite side of the lane behind post man 5. The post man on the clearout side cuts up to the high post just outside the free-throw lane area. He may receive a pass from the point man or set a stationary screen so that 1 can brush off his defensive man and drive to the basket or shoot the jump shot (Diagram 2-1).

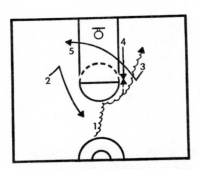

Diagram 2-1. Clear with Dribble Entry.

Note: Our point man has been taught a variety of offensive maneuvers in order to be able to beat his defensive man. We teach him the cross-over, stutter, reverse or whirl, stop-and-go moves, plus how to use each of these moves to beat his man. We also teach him how to vary the tempo of his approach to further keep his defensive man off balance. This is the key to success of all half-court offensive options.

The Clear Option begins with the pass from point man 1 to the post man 4 (Diagram 2-2). After passing, 1 jab-steps to his left and cuts back to his right to get a return pass from 4. Upon receiving the ball, the point man may immediately shoot the quick jump shot, drive to the right, all the time looking for a good shot, or may pass to 4 who rolls out to the basket after passing the ball back to 1.

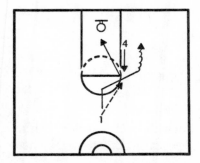

Diagram 2-2. Clear with Pass Entry.

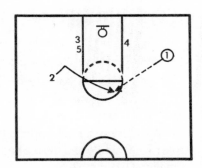

Diagram 2-3. To Change Sides.

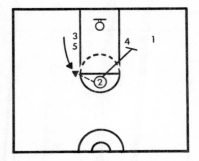

Diagram 2-4. Automatic Swing.

Diagram 2-5. Options for 3.

Note: The post man 4 should guard against the offensive charge on the rollout by off-side defensive men. To counter this tactic, we added the quick Swing Option back to the opposite side of the court.

If 1 does not get the high-percentage shot on the drive or the jump shot or does not elect to hit the roll-out man 4, he passes to 2 who has cut from behind a double screen set by 3 and 5 to a position near the free-throw line. 2 may shoot or drive if open or run the automatic Swing Option (Diagram 2-3).

Upon seeing the ball being passed to 2, 3 immediately cuts around post man 5 for a possible pass from 2 (Diagram 2-4). 3 may shoot, drive into the lane or back to the left, or hit post man 5 with a pass (Diagram 2-5). 2, after passing to 3, screens away from the ball for 1 (Diagram 2-7).

Options for 3 (Diagram 2-5):

    1. Shoot upon receiving the ball;

    2. Drive the middle and shoot;

    3. Drive back to the left and shoot; or

    4. Pass to 5.

A highly successful option for the team with a tall post man (5) is to drive to the middle and lob the ball to the tall post man if a defensive switch is made (Diagram 2-6).

After passing to 3, 2 screens away from the ball for 1 who cuts to the free-throw line (Diagram 2-7).

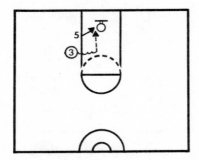
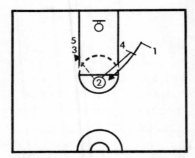

Diagram 2-6. Drive Middle,   **Diagram 2-7. Screen by 2.**
Lob Pass to 5.

Seldom do we have to use all of these options to obtain a high percentage shot. If we need additional options, we can continue setting the Swing Options back to the weak or off side or we can go into a Three-Man Weave pattern (Diagram 2-8). Instead of hitting Swing man 3, 2 initiates the weave pattern by dribbling toward 3 and handing off as 3 cuts into the lane. 3 may shoot or continue on across the lane to hand off to 1.

To clearout the left-wing guard 2, the point man either waves him through or calls his name and tells him to clear. 2 takes a jab step toward 1 and quickly reverses to the basket. If 2 does not receive a pass from 1, he sets up on the opposite side of the lane behind post man 4. The post man on the clearout side moves up to the high post just outside the free-throw lane.

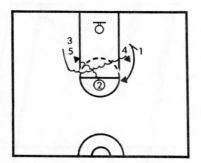

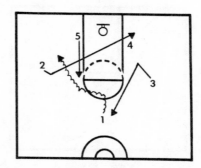

Diagram 2-8. Three-Man Weave.

Diagram 2-9. Left Wing Guard Clearout.

He may receive a pass from 1 or set a stationary screen so 1 can brush his defensive man off and drive to the basket or shoot the jump shot. 3 is assigned to be the defensive safety man guarding against the fast break in case of a turnover (Diagram 2-9).

After signaling 2 to clear, 1 passes to 5 and cuts to get open. In Diagram 2-10, 1 receives a return pass from 5 and drives toward the baseline. He can drive all the way to the basket, if open, or may pass to 5 who rolls to the basket. Teams that switch automatically are susceptible to the roll-out play.

If 1 does not get the desired shots or pass to the roll man 5, 3 cuts sharply to the ball to receive a pass from 1. After receiving the ball from 1, 3 immediately pivots to face the basket. 3 may shoot, drive, or run the Swing Option back to the weak side (Diagram 2-11).

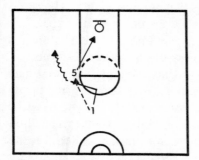

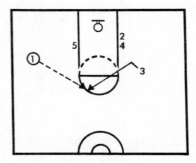

Diagram 2-10. Pick and Roll Option (Clearout Side).

Diagram 2-11. To Change Sides.

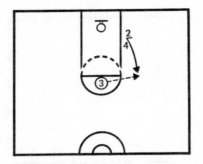

Diagram 2-12. Automatic Swing.   Diagram 2-13. Options for 2.

As 3 receives the ball, 2 swings or pops out from behind the screen being set by post man 4. 3 hits 2 with a pass and screens away (Diagram 2-12).

Options for 2 (Diagram 2-13):

1. Shoot upon receiving the pass;
2. Drive the middle and shoot;
3. Drive the baseline and shoot;
4. Pass to post man 4 and cut
5. Pass to 1, cutting from the weak side; or
6. Run the drive and lob to post man 4.

After passing to 2 (Diagram 2-11), 3 sets a screen with 5 for the off side guard 1 (Diagram 2-14). *Note:* This play is delayed until 2 has used the options available to him. We tell our players that it is better to be late than too early on all of the off-side options. Cutting to the ball before 2 is ready to pass, eliminates the effectiveness of the off-side options.

This play starts just like the Regular Clear Option. The point man calls "4 Clear." 4 cuts to a high post position just outside the free-throw lane and 3 jab-steps and reverses to the basket quickly (Diagram 2-15). This deception is what causes the play to be effective. 4 cuts to a position behind post man 5 and 3, instead of clearing across the lane as he did on the Regular Clear Option, cuts to the high post spot vacated by 4. 1 now may use 3 as a screener (Diagram 2-16), hit 3 with a pass and cut around for a return pass (Diagram 2-17) or may screen away.

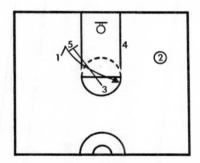

Diagram 2-14. Screen Away by 3.

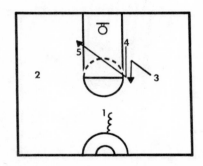

Diagram 2-15. The "4" Clear Option.

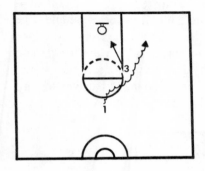

Diagram 2-16.

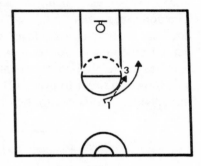

Diagram 2-17.

Note: This option is excellent for the team that has a wing man with outstanding one-on-one ability. If a coach is a strong advocate of one-on-one basketball, this option is an excellent play.

To effectively teach the wing men to get the maximum results from this option, we drill them daily on the various one-on-one moves.

To change sides, pass the ball to 2 who has cut to free-throw lane area (Diagram 2-18). 2 may shoot, drive, or run the Automatic Swing Option (Diagram 2-19) with 4 and 5.

As 2 receives the ball, 4 swings around 5 for a pass from 2 (Diagram 2-19). 4 has the same options as all of the bottom men cutting off the Swing Options. 4 may shoot, drive or pass to 5 on the pick-and-roll.

The final play of the Clearout Series is "5 Clear", which is the

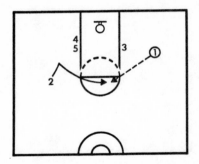

Diagram 2-18. To Change Sides.

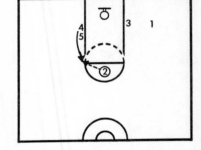

Diagram 2-19. Automatic Swing.

mirror of ''4 Clear'' using the 5 man as the clearout man, rather than 4. The point man calls ''5 Clear''. 5 cuts to a high post position and if he does not receive a pass, clears to a position across the free-throw lane behind post man 4. As soon as 5 clears out, 2 cuts to the basket and reverses to the high post spot vacated by 5. 1 may pass to 2 or use him as a screen in order to brush off his defensive man. If 1 drives toward the outside, 2 rolls out to the basket (Diagram 2-20).

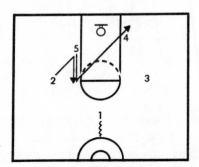

Diagram 2-20. The "5" Clear Option

To change the ball quickly to the weak side to run the Swing Option, 1 passes to 3 who has cut to the free-throw lane area (Diagram 2-21). The Automatic Swing play may be run with 5 cutting around 4 for a quick pass from 3 (Diagram 2-22).

Note: The key to all the Swing Options is to swing out just as the man at the free-throw lane receives the ball. Players have a tendency to swing

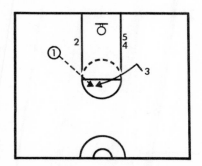 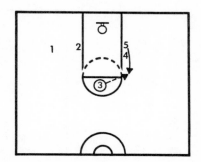

Diagram 2-21. To Change Sides. **Diagram 2-22. Automatic Swing.**

before the passer gets the ball at this point. We teach our players to delay this cut. It is better to be late than too early. The quickness with which the ball is reversed also adds to the pattern's success or failure.

This series has been highly successful for us in obtaining high-percentage shots. The Clearout Series may be used as the primary offense or as a part of the multiple offensive setup. It can also be used to get the ball to a specific player at any time during the course of a ball game.

REBOUNDING PATTERNS AND DEFENSIVE SAFETY ASSIGNMENTS

Among the features of the 1-2-2 offense that the author feels are highly important are its rebounding patterns. The 1-2-2 puts men closer to the basket than do many of the other conventional 2-1-2 patterns used at all levels of basketball.

Our basic theory of rebounding is always to have a rebounding triangle at the basket. We want men on each side of the basket and at least one in front of the basket. A fourth man may rebound, attempt to tie up the opponent's rebounder, or drop back to an assigned secondary rebounding position. Diagram 2-23 shows this rebounding triangle.

Rebounders 3, 4 and 5 form the basic triangle in this diagram. 1 can go to the free-throw line to become a secondary rebounder, go to the ball and help prevent the outlet pass if the opponents get the ball, or he may drop back to help 2 with the defensive safety assignment.

Note: The defensive safety never lets an opponent get behind him.

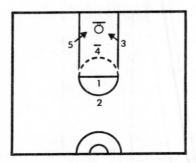

Diagram 2-23. Rebound Triangle.

To stress this to our players, the safety man who lets a man get behind him automatically comes out ot the game. We do not do this for any other mistake except loafing down the floor.

The following diagrams will show the rebounding and safety assignments on the four main options presented in this chapter.

In these diagrams, R designates the rebounder and S the safety man. If the shot is taken by 1, 3 and 5 become the off-side rebounders and the front rebounder. 4 will form the triangle on the ball side. As soon as the ball is shot we want these men going for the board to try to get the inside spots on the defensive men (Diagram 2-24). 1 can go to the previously mentioned assignments while 2 is the main defensive safety man. If the opponents get the rebound, then our nearest rebounder to the ball is

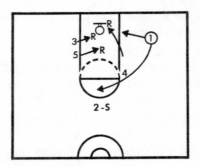

Diagram 2-24. Rebound-Safety Pattern for Regular Clear Option.

instructed to prevent the quick outlet pass as our other players move to their respective defensive assignments.

A coach may have to vary his rebounding patterns to counter a specific opponent's strategy. A few years ago in the Tennessee State Tournament, we took an unheralded team against a heavily-favored Chattanooga Howard team. This opponent was one of the pre-tourney favorites. We had an excellent scouting report which showed they liked either to make a rather long outlet pass to a guard at the mid-court line or to throw a long pass down court. Our strategy was to assign our smallest two guards to the opponent's two guards as soon as we shot. Our two post men would then battle on the boards and the remaining man would go to the potential rebounder and prevent the outlet pass.

We had 16 interceptions during the first two quarters and held the opponents to 18 points at the end of the half while scoring 36 of our own.

Diagram 2-25 shows the Rebound-Safety Pattern on the Option to Clear the Left Wing Guard. On a shot by 1 or 5, 2 and 4 take the off-side and front spots. 5 fills the ball-side spot and 1 carries out the pre-arranged assignment. 3 is the safety man.

Diagram 2-26 shows the Rebound-Safety Pattern for the Option 4 Clear. 4 and 5 take the off-side and front positions and 3 fills the ball-side spot. 1 goes to his pre-assigned position.

Note: One of the features of this series is that there are two rebounders on the off side away from where the shot is taken. This gives the offensive team a better chance at obtaining the second and third shot if it is needed.

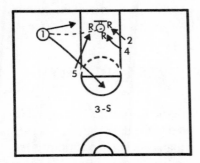 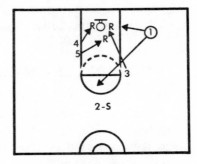

Diagram 2-25. Rebound-Safety Pattern for Clearout Left Wing Guard.   Diagram 2-26. Rebound-Safety Pattern for 4 Clear.

On the shot by 1 or 2, 4 and 5 assume the off-side and front rebound positions. 2 fills the ball-side spot while 1 goes to his pre-assigned spot. 3 is the safety man (Diagram 2-27).

Diagram 2-27. Rebound-Safety Pattern for 5 Clear.

Note: The rebounders in the triangle are drilled to keep moving in order to keep from being boxed out. They are taught to keep the ball alive on the basket, even if just tipping with one hand. Much leeway is given in the area of offensive rebounding. The author feels the offensive rebounders can crash the boards with reckless abandon as long as they do not go over the defensive rebounders' backs and fewer fouls will be called on the offensive men.

Note: Rebounding is a key factor in a team's success and the author feels that most teams do not spend enough time on this phase of the game.

HOW TO USE THE CLEAROUT SERIES EFFECTIVELY

The key to using the Clearout Series effectively is the point man. He must be able to handle the basketball and get it to the designated position, to use the screens properly, or to pass to the man moving in position either to receive a pass or screen. To be doubly effective, the point man should be a good jump shooter.

When we first installed the 1-2-2 Clearout Series, we had a great point man by the name of Jimmy England. He was an All-State and All-American high school performer and later became one of the greatest one-on-one players in the Southeastern Conference at the University of Tennessee. He also made some of the All-American selections while there. Of course, a coach doesn't have a player of this caliber every year, but we have had a lot of success with players of lesser ability at the point. The key, then, is to know the strengths and limitations of the point man and use his assets to the fullest.

Prior to coming to Oak Ridge, in 12 years I had only two players over 6′ 4″ (both were 6′ 5″), so height or lack of it does not prevent a coach from using the 1-2-2 offense effectively with two post men.

Only parts of the series may be selected for use. An example of this is when a coach wants a specific player to have the ball for a last-second shot or for a key basket. Simply select the option in the Clearout Series that gets the ball to that particular player.

Therefore, effective use of this series depends on knowing the talent you have on hand. Then, choose the corresponding option to utilize the available talent.

CHAPTER 3

Expanding the 1-2-2 Offense
with the Exchange Series

The Exchange Series is a group of play options revolving around the interchanging of positions by wing guards and post men. The need for this interchanging was brought about by several factors which are to be discussed below.

To Give Additional Movement to the Basic 1-2-2

Perhaps one of the most important reasons for the development and addition of the Exchange Series to the 1-2-2 system, initially, was to give the offense more movement. Offensive movement is a must in developing a sound attack and the Exchange Series aids in this area.

To Counter Pressure on Entry Passes

The second factor for adding the Exchange Series was because of strong pressure on our two wing guards by teams with quicker defensive men than our offensive wing guards. Even though we drilled regularly on how to get open to receive the ball at the desired position on the wing, we still encountered problems when we used bigger and slower wing guards. The Exchange Series helped diminish our problems with the entry passes.

Provides High Percentage Shots

All options in the Exchange Series will provide shots inside the 15-foot range. A shot outside this area is completely unnecessary and the coach should constantly stress this point.

Many Screens Available

The most difficult problems a defense must face are the offenses that combine screening with constant player movement. The Exchange Series utilizes this factor by creating multiple screens with player movement, thus forcing opponents into switching situations which can be highly confusing to players at all levels of competition.

The Exchange Series uses strong-side and weak-side screens together to help confuse the defense and keep it off balance. The weak-side swing options are highly difficult to stop and produce many excellent scoring opportunities.

Continuity Always Present

The author strongly believes in the continuity principle on offense. By this principle, an offense may be run to either side and back without having to reset the players each time a certain phase of the offense is run that doesn't provide a good shot. The Exchange Series, especially 43 and 52 Exchanges, adhere strictly to this principle of offense.

Mismatches May be Created

Creating mismatches either by posting big guards on smaller defensive guards in the low post area or taking the opponent's big man outside are two highly successful offensive techniques used by top high school, college and professional teams. The Exchange Series accomplishes both of these techniques on the initial options. Even if the opponents employ switching techniques on the initial entry exchanges, they will be caught on the weak-side swing option or the reverse-and-go opposite techniques which will be shown later in this chapter.

To Give the Offense More Options

The final reason for adding the Exchange Series is simply to give the 1-2-2 offense more options for the defensive team to try to stop. We might save the Exchange Series for the third or fourth quarters or use it only as a change of pace when the basic 1-2-2 options are not working as well as expected.

Changing to the Series during a crucial time has broken games wide open and provided some big wins. For these reasons we believe in the Exchange Series as a highly effective set of offensive options that can be utilized at all levels of competition.

43 Exchange. To initiate the first option on the Exchange Series, the point man 1 calls "43" as he approaches the top of the circle on the offensive end of the court (Diagram 3- 1). Upon hearing the call, 3 moves down to set a screen on 4's defensive man. 4 then breaks out to the wing guard position vacated by 3 to receive a pass from 1. 3 moves on across the lane area after his screen for 4. He will form a second screen with 5 on the side opposite the free-throw lane for 2.

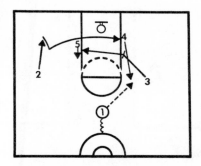

Diagram 3-1.

As soon as the entry pass is made from 1 to 4, 2 moves down toward the baseline. The purpose of this maneuver is to position 2's defensive man so he will have to fight through the double screen being established by 3 and 5. 2 may now cut along the baseline to the basket looking for a pass from 4. The key to scoring an easy basket on this play is the way 2 sets up his defensive man. He must casually walk his man down toward the baseline area where his defensive man may be caught in the double screen. Then, with the ball in 4's possession, 2 cuts quickly behind the double screen. A good fake should precede the cut by 2.

A second method of initiating the 43 Exchange option is to call the Exchange Series at a time out or during a free-throw situation. The point man will dribble the ball to the right side of the circle. As soon as 1 gets in a position to make the entry pass, 3 will set the screen on 4. This optional plan may be necessary because of the problem of crowd noise in many high school gyms. Oral signals are often difficult to hear and hand signals are not possible if the point man is being pressured, so this method may be desirable.

The Swing Counter option provides a quick pop-out play and helps counter sagging defenses. Diagram 3-2 shows the continuity to the weak side if the first shot option does not provide the desired results. 4 passes back out to 1. 1 must set up his cut to the ball by faking away from 4 toward the basket. 4 passes to 1. As soon as 1 gets the ball, 3 cuts around 5 to receive a pass from 1. 3 may shoot the quick jump shot if open or pass to 5. 3 can also drive. See Diagram 3-3 for a breakdown of the Swing option.

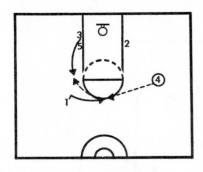

Diagram 3-2.

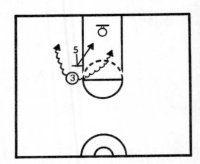

Diagram 3-3.

If 3 does not shoot after receiving the pass from 1, he may work with 5 either by passing to 5 or using him as a screener. 5 may screen for 3 as 3 drives either toward the middle of the lane or to the baseline. 5 rolls out to the basket for a possible pass from 3 for the pick-and-roll play (Diagram 3-3). Caution must be taken by the screener 5 to screen legally. Post screens are carefully scrutinized by the officials and the coach should constantly teach the proper screening techniques.

This Swing option is quite an effective play if a team has a big man. The option clears out much of the support from the opposite side of the court because of the quickness of the play and opening up of the weak side for the Swing play. Also, there are no opponents on the weak side to help cut off the play. This is especially true if 3 drives to the middle instead of back to the baseline.

If for some reason 3 does not get the ball from 1 on the Swing option, he may cut over the top of 5 to the basket (Diagram 3-4). Then 5 will step in to the lane to receive a pass from 1 and have a short shot to the basket. 5

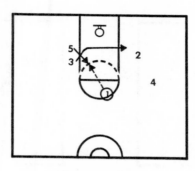

Diagram 3-4.

may fake to the inside and drop-step to the basket for the power lay-up or the hook shot. The Step In maneuver is an excellent way to get the ball into the low post man. When facing teams that switch automatically on screening situations, a mismatch can be created by putting the wing guard with the smallest defensive man on him at the 3 spot. Thus, when the opponent's post man switches to cover 3, the mismatch occurs. 1 then passes to 5 who should be able to overpower the opponent's defensive guard. I firmly advocate getting the ball inside and making the opponent's big men play defense. Many coaches, when playing an opponent with a big post man, tend to rely on the outside options and try to outshoot them from the outside. Our offensive philosophy is to take the ball to the highest percentage areas and try to score from there. If we cannot match our opponents in height, we create more movement. This movement opens up the high-percentage scoring options, enabling us to counteract any height disadvantage incurred.

Diagram 3-5 illustrates a Double Swing option that may be used effectively. This option is a continuation play that does not have to be called by the point man after his initial exchange call. 4 passes back to 1 at the top of the free-throw circle and screens down on 2's defensive man. As soon as the pass went from 4 to 1, 3 cut around 5 for the weak-side Swing described in Diagrams 3-2, 3-3 and 3-4. The 4 and 2 Swing may be slightly delayed to allow the 3 and 5 plays to develop. Since both plays are quick hitting options, there will be very little delay and a continuous pattern should occur.

If a good shot has not been obtained by the time all of the options described have been used, we will run the "Pick for One" option shown in

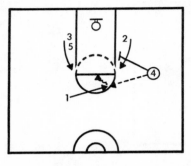

Diagram 3-5.

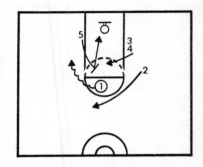

Diagram 3-6.

Diagram 3-6. This option may go to either side, but is more effective if run to the side where the Swing man has gone over the top of the screen and cut to the middle to the other side. Instead of receiving a pass on the Step In option, 5 sets a screen on 1's defensive man. This must be done quickly to avoid a three-second violation.

1 looks for the drive or the quick jump shot after dribbling off the screen by 5. 4 cuts to the free-throw line area in order to keep his defensive man occupied so the Screen and Roll by 5 may develop. The Roll out by 5 is primarily for securing rebounding position on the offensive board and 5 should be careful not to incur the offensive foul on the roll out. 2 rotates out front to act as the safety man and/or to help 1 reset the offense in case a shot was not taken (Diagram 3-6).

Reverse and Go Opposite Option. Occasionally, the defensive man covering 1 will deny the pass from 4 to 1 by getting between 1 and 4. When this happens, 1 pushes off on his right foot, pivots or reverses to the basket for a backdoor cut. 1 fills in the spot vacated by 3 who replaced 1 out front. 3 cuts around 5 to meet the pass from 4 and may trigger the Swing option between 1 and 5. This option is called Reverse and Go Opposite (Diagram 3-7).

Swing Option with 1 Replacing 3. Diagram 3-8 shows the Swing option after 1 has reversed and cut opposite to fill the 3 spot behind 5. 3 has cut to be the ball handler on the option. 4 passes to 3. As the pass is completed, 1 breaks around 5 and may receive a pass from 3 and run the Swing option. 1 may also shoot the quick jump shot after receiving the pass from 3.

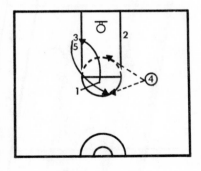

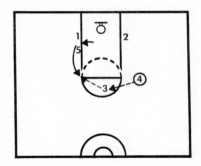

Diagram 3-7.   Diagram 3-8.

52 Exchange. To begin the second option on the Exchange Series, 1 calls ''52'' as he approaches the top of the circle on the offensive end of the floor. After hearing the call by 1, wing guard 2 cuts to screen 5's defensive man. 5 fakes into the lane with a jab step and cuts out to the left wing position using the screen set by 2. 5 may shoot the quick jump shot or may pass to 2 who has established a low post position after his screen. This maneuver by 2 is called posting a guard and may be used when the wing guard 2 is being guarded by a much shorter defensive man. This maneuver, although relatively simple, is a highly effective offensive technique.

If 5 does not shoot or pass to 2, 2 will move on across the lane and set a second screen with 4. 4 moves up the lane a step to make room for 2's screen.

In the meantime, 3 walks his man down to a position where he can rub him off on the double screen by 2 and 4. 3 cuts along the baseline and looks for a possible pass from 5 (Diagram 3-9). 5 may also use the cleared area to drive and use his individual offensive moves to score.

Swing Counter Option. If a shot has not developed from the entry pass to 5, 1 fakes to his right and cuts to receive a pass from 5. As soon as 1 receives the ball from 5, 2 cuts around 4's screen for a possible pass from 1. 2 can shoot, drive to the middle, drive to the base line, or pass to 4 on the inside.

The Double Swing Option may be run simultaneously with the Swing Option between 2 and 4 (Diagram 3-11). The Double Swing Option may be used without any call by the point men. After 5 passes the

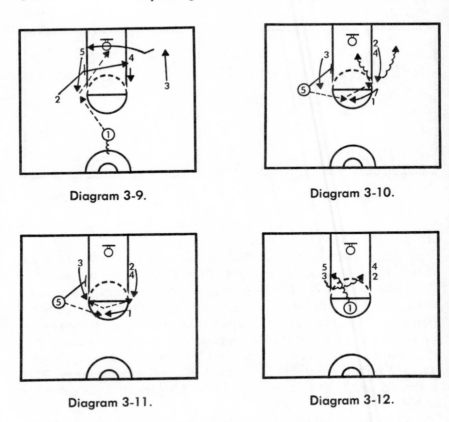

Diagram 3-9.   Diagram 3-10.

Diagram 3-11.   Diagram 3-12.

ball to 1 for the weak side or off-side Swing option, 5 screens down the lane on 3's defensive man. 3 will cut around 5 for a possible pass from 1.

This will be a delayed Swing option since the 2.4 Swing will have been started a few seconds before. However, the delay will give 1 a chance to decide whether 2 is open on the weak side or if he has a shot himself. 1 may then pass to 3 on the left side.

Another effective maneuver is shown in Diagram 3-12. 1 begins a dribble weave to either direction. 3, after receiving a pass from 1, may shoot or continue the dribble weave by handing off to 2.

The Step-In Option. If 2 did not receive a pass after the Swing option, 2 cuts over the top of 4 to the other side of the court. 1 then passes to 4 who is now isolated one-on-one on the right side of the lane. This option provides an excellent opportunity for the team that

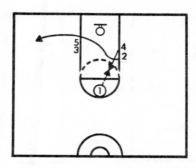

Diagram 3-13.

has a post man who is a good one-on-one player. 1 can hold his position after passing to 4, go screen for 3, or cut outside 4 for a possible return pass (Diagram 3-13).

All post men are drilled almost daily on one-on-one maneuvers to take advantage of any isolation option. The post men go through these offensive moves during the free shooting period at the beginning of practice.

45 Exchange. The previous two Exchange options involved an interchange between the wing guards and the post men (43 and 52 Exchange). Options 45 and 54 involve screens by one post man for the other post man. The post exchanges were added to the series when we had two good offensive post men who were good ball handlers and could also drive to the basket very well.

Diagram 3-14 shows the 45 Exchange Option. 1 begins the play by calling "45." 4, upon hearing the call, cuts to the free-throw line for a possible pass from 1. Generally, 4 will not be open and this is a decoy move to set up the next screen. However, if 1 does get the pass to 4, 4 turns and faces the basket. He may shoot, step, fake and shoot, drive to the basket, or pass to 5 on the inside option (See Diagram 3-15). 1 must keep his defensive man occupied by cutting away from the ball. Wing guards 2 and 3 cut to a wide baseline position. This serves to help keep the middle area open for the post men so they have room to operate their two man options.

If 4 did not receive a pass from 1, 4 will move down the free-throw lane and set a screen on 5's defensive man. 5 must help set up the screen by stepping into the lane to fake going across the lane. 5 cuts the the

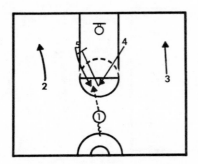 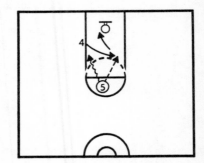

Diagram 3-14.   **Diagram 3-15.**

free-throw line for a possible pass from 1 (Diagram 3-14). As soon as he receives the ball, he may shoot, drive, or pass to screener 4 on the inside option (Diagram 3-15).

On the Inside option, 5, after receiving the ball, faces the basket. He may shoot or pass to the other post man 4 who, after screening for 5, rolls back inside the lane. If 4 is a fairly good offensive post man, he will be able to get an excellent shot near the basket.

Quick movement through the lane should be stressed to avoid the three-second violation. After the screen by 4, he must step out of the free-throw lane area so he will have the full three seconds to make his cut into the lane.

A second cut is available to 4 at this point. 4 may begin his inside cut across the lane. If the defensive man is forcing 4 hard on the cut, reverse-cut back to the side from which 4's cut began. 5 may hit 4 for a drop step and a hook or power lay-up may be available.

Sideline Pick Down Option. The Outside option is available after 1 passes to 5. As the post men are working the inside options, 1 screens for the wing guard 3. 3 fakes toward the basket to set up the cut behind the screen being set by 1. 3 immediately looks for a pass from the post man with the ball and may shoot or drive to the basket, still looking for the shot. 2 rotates out front to become the defensive safety. 5, after passing to 3, either rolls down the lane or screens for 3, driving off the first screen by 1 (Diagram 3-16).

The Sideline Pick Down option is good for a team having a left-handed wing guard in the 3 wing-guard position.

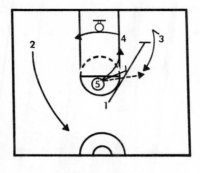

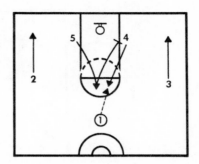

Diagram 3-16.   Diagram 3-17.

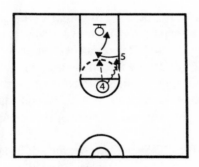

Diagram 3-18.

54 Exchange. The second post option is called "54 Exchange" (Diagram 3-17). 1 calls "54." 5 cuts to the free-throw line for a possible pass from 1. If 5 receives the ball, he may shoot, step, fake and shoot, drive or pass to 4 on the inside option. If 5 is unable to receive a pass from 1, 5 moves down to screen for 4. 4 sets up the screen being set by 5 by stepping into the lane. Then, as the screener arrives, 4 cuts to the free-throw line. 1 will pass to 4 if he is open. 4 may shoot, drive, or pass to the 5 man (Diagram 3-18).

Diagram 3-18 shows the inside option if 4 received the ball from 1 at the free throw line. 5 cuts across the lane area looking for a pass from 4. 5 may also use the cut-back maneuver previously described in the 45 Exchange option. 4 passes to 5 who works his man one-on-one. 4 may drive if he does not pass to 5. 5's cut clears the area for 4's drive.

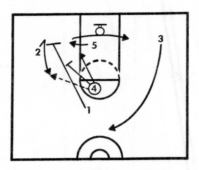

Diagram 3-19.

The third phase of the 54 Exchange option is the outside play (Diagram 3-19). 1, after passing to 4, moves away toward the baseline and screens for the wing guard 2. 2 fakes a cut toward the basket to set up the screen by 1. After 2 cuts off the screen, he immediately looks for the pass from 4 and a possible shot or drive to the basket. 2 may pass to 4, cutting inside, or use an optional screen set by 4 just outside the lane. 3 rotates out front to become the defensive safety man or release man if the shot is not obtained.

The sideline Pick Down Options, in addition to being scoring options, help keep the defensive guards from helping in the middle area. We have found these options to be very difficult for our opposition to defend against, especially when we are operating with two quick post men who are good one-on-one and two-on-two players.

OFFENSIVE REBOUNDING AND SAFETY ASSIGNMENTS

Diagram 3-20 shows the rebounding and defensive safety positions for the 43 Exchange Option shown in Offensive Diagram 3-1. On a shot by 2 on the first baseline cut, 3 fills the off-side low position; 5 fills the front position; 2 covers the low ball-side spot, and 4 rebounds in the front position on ball side or goes to the outlet safety position. 1 rotates to the outside to become the defensive safety man.

If we are employing the 3-2 rebound philosophy (three men rebounding—two men in dual safety), 4, being further from the basket than 2, 3 or 5, takes the dual safety position. In our rebounding

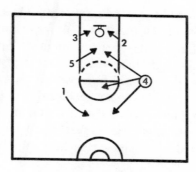

Diagram 3-20.

philosophy, we always want two men going to the basket on the side of the basket opposite the shot. This factor is very important and must be constantly stressed by the coaching staff if a team is to be highly successful in obtaining the second and third shots necessary for playing winning basketball.

This rebounding philosophy has enabled our much smaller teams to consistently out-rebound bigger and taller opponents. One of our teams, playing with 6' 1" and 6' 2-½" post men, upset the state's number-one ranked team by dominating the rebounding department against 6' 4" and 6' 5" opponents.

Diagram 3-21 illustrates the rebounding and defensive safety assignments for the Swing option off the 43 Exchange play shown in diagram 3-2. On a shot by 3 on the Swing option, 2 covers the off-side low position; 4 fills the front rebounding spot; 5 rebounds the low ball-side

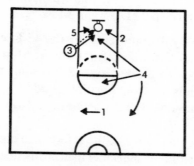

Diagram 3-21.

position; 3 follows his shot. 1 is the safety man. On this option, we will usually gamble by sending 4 to the off-side front position because we want at least two men on the off-side rebound. Our main reason for employing this off-side rebounding technique is because most missed shots come off on the opposite side of the board from which the shot was taken.

Also, most teams we play do not get the outlet pass out as well to the right side as they do if the rebound comes off on the left. Because most players are right-handed, it is easier to get the ball out to the left. We feel the gamble is worth risking and have been hurt only on rare occasions by the outlet pass to the right.

3 is told to recover quickly to help 1 on the safety assignment if he sees the opponents secure the rebound on the opposite side.

Rebound and Safety Pattern for 52 Exchange, 1st Option. (See Offensive Diagram 3-9.) On a baseline shot by 3, 2 rebounds the low off-side position; 4 rebounds the off-side front position; 3 covers the ball-side low position; 5 either rebounds on ball-side front, covers the outlet spot at the free-throw line, or drops back to the dual safety position. 1 becomes the safety man (Diagram 3-22). Remember, 1 must never let an opponent receive a pass behind him. A violation of this rule is punished immediately by substituting for the 1 man who allowed the opponents to get behind him.

Rebound and Safety Pattern for the Swing Option, 52 Exchange. (See Offensive Diagram 3-10.) 2 shoots off of the Swing option. 3 rebounds the low off-side spot. 5 covers the off-side front position. Here again we will send the safety man to the board as described above. 2 rebounds the front position on the ball side or may help 1 with the dual safety position. If we get hurt on the assignment of 5, we will send him to the dual safety spot (Diagram 3-23).

Rebound Safety Assignments for the 45 Exchange. (See Offensive Diagram 3-14.) On a shot from the free-throw line by 5, 4 rebounds the low spot on the left side; 3 rebounds the low spot on the right side; 2 rebounds the front position as does 5. 2 may retreat to the dual safety position as does 1. The outside man always stays out to become the safety man.

In a dual safety assignment, the safety man on the ball side may be assigned the job of stopping the outlet man on his side of the court with the other dual safety preventing any opponent from getting behind him.

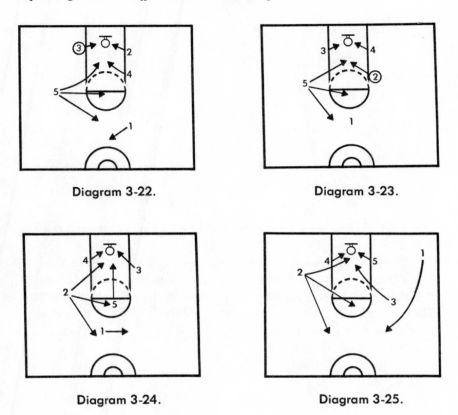

Diagram 3-22.

Diagram 3-23.

Diagram 3-24.

Diagram 3-25.

Diagram 3-25 shows the *rebounding and safety assignments for the Sideline Pick Down Option*. (See Offensive Diagram 3-16.) On a shot by 3, 4 rebounds the low off-side position; 5 the low ball-side spot; 2 fills the off-side front position; 3 follows his shot or helps with the dual safety assignment; while 1 rotates out front for the safety assignment.

Diagram 3-26 illustrates the *rebound and safety assignments for the 54 Exchange Option*. (See Offensive Diagram 3-17.) On a shot by 4, 2 rebounds the low off-side position; 5 covers the low right-side position; 4 rebounds in the front position; 3 either rebounds or fills the dual safety position; 1 remains out front to fill the safety position.

When the ball is shot from the free-throw line it is more difficult to rebound two men on the off-side since it is often impossible to determine

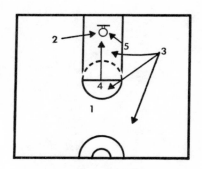

Diagram 3-26.

Diagram 3-27.

which side will be the off side. We will invoke the 3-2 rebound rule on these shots.

The *rebounding and defensive safety assignments for the Sideline Pick Option off the 54 Exchange* are shown in 3-27. (See Offensive Diagram 3-19.) On a shot by 2, 5 rebounds the off-side position; 4 rebounds the low ball-side position; 3 either fills the front rebound position or drops back to dual safety; 2 follows his shot in front and 1 rotates to the safety position.

CHAPTER 4

Adding the Stack Series
to the 1-2-2 Offense

The Stack Offensive Series is composed of five basic plays which have five basic options off each play. These five plays are:

1. The Double Screen Option.
2. The Pick and Roll Option.
3. The One-on-One Isolation Option.
4. The Baseline Cutter Option.
5. The Double Swing Option.

Consequently, if all five basic plays are used with all five different players there are 25 ways to score from the Stack Series.

The Stack Series Options are all predetermined set plays and fit into an offensive system that is highly play-conscious. The plays are exceptionally good for the highly mechanized teams whose coach wants to know where every player is when the ball is at a certain point on the floor.

The Stack Series may be used totally, or the coach may select only the options to fit one or two top players. For example, play option No. 2 is excellent for the team that has an outstanding jump shooter who needs the double screen to get open. This same option may be used to get the good shot at the end-of-the-quarter play or at the end of the game.

The options may be called to create an isolation situation for a good one-on-one man. Options are presented that will get all four men (except the point man) into isolated situations.

63

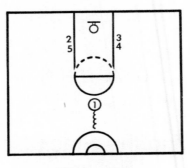

Diagram 4-1.

The basic alignment for the Stack Series is shown in Diagram 4-1. The wing guards, 2 and 3, set up in a position behind the post men, 4 and 5, in what we refer to as the "Stack" or "Double Stack" position. We have also used the word "Tight" to designate the same formation.

Both wing men (2 and 3) help the point man (1) bring the ball up the court. If we face full court man-to-man pressure, we get the ball to the point man and get out of his way. The wing guards are told to clear on up the court, but always to keep the point man in view in case he needs help.

We advocate bringing the ball up the court in a one-on-one fashion. Each of our players is drilled in techniques of getting the ball up the floor in this manner. One season, one of our post men was the best ball handler on the team, so he would bring the ball down as a guard and we would run a release pattern to get him into the desired post position because of his rebounding and shooting ability.

In our pre-season practice sessions, all players must go through the full-court dribbling and ball-handling drills to develop the ball-handling techniques necessary for handling full-court pressure. We have found that many of our 6'3" or 6'4" post men in high school become guards in college, so it is our responsibility to help our players prepare for future competition. This fundamental ball-handling development is just one of the ways we fulfill this responsibility.

The No. 2 Play. Diagram 4-2 shows the first play in the Stack Series. The option is keyed by the point man 1 calling "Stack." If we are in our regular 1-2-2 alignment, the two wing guards line up below the post men on their respective sides of the court. The coach may have the team just line up in the Stack positions as the point man advances into the offensive

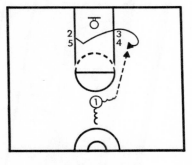

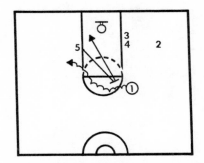

Diagram 4-2.   Diagram 4-3.

end of the court. Then, 1 will call the play number (in this case No. 2). This is the double screen for the wing guard 2.

The point man 1 is instructed to keep his dribble going as he moves over to complete the first option (Diagram 4-2). If 2 is not open, 1 crosses over and dribbles back to his left, anticipating a screen from 5 near the free throw line (Diagram 4-3). 5 sets a stationary screen on 1's defensive man. 1, after driving around 3's screen, looks for a shot or a possible pass to 5, who rolls out to the basket. The roll out by 5 is more to the left side of the free-throw lane than directly to the basket because the defensive men covering 3 and 4 should be in the lane as defensive help or support men. The offensive foul on the roll out is a problem that must be avoided and the roll out to the left side will help solve the foul problem. 2 rotates out to become the defensive safety man if a shot occurs by either 1 or 5.

The third play in this series is the isolation option. Diagram 4-4 illustrates what happens if 1 decides to pass the ball back to the weak side where only 5 is located. This is a tremendous option for a good driving post man with excellent one-on-one offensive skills. 1 passes the ball to 5 and remains on the same side from which he passed the ball. This creates an isolation for 5, who has the entire left side of the court to maneuver one-on-one.

The fourth play in the series is the baseline cutter option. If 1 has used the pick-and-roll option and a good shot was not obtained, 5 will continue across the lane and set up a double screen with 4 for 2 who fakes and cuts along the baseline for a possible pass from 1. 3 rotates out front for defensive safety purposes and to be in position for the next option in the Series (Diagram 4-5).

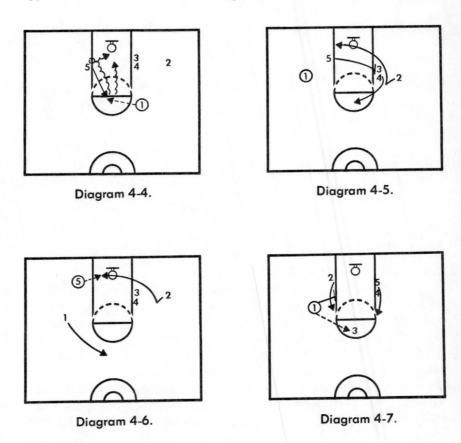

Diagram 4-4.   Diagram 4-5.

Diagram 4-6.   Diagram 4-7.

Diagram 4-6 shows the baseline option if 1 passes to 5 on the isolation option. 3 and 4 set a double screen for 2 who cuts along the baseline for a possible pass from 5 and a shot.

The fifth play in the Stack sequence is the double swing option shown in Diagram 4-7. The Double Swing is the final option and results if 1 does not shoot or pass to 5 on the Baseline Cutter option shown in Diagram 4-5. 3 receives a pass from 1 at the free-throw line. After passing, 1 moves to a position near the free-throw lane to set a screen for 2 who fakes toward the basket and cuts around the screen by 1. Meanwhile, 5 cuts around 4, looking for a possible pass from 3.

3 has the option to shoot, pass to 1, or pass to 5. 3 may also initiate the Dribble Weave pattern.

1 and 5 should be ready to step toward the basket if a switch occurs

between their man and the man swinging around the screen. If teams are not adept at switching consistently, an easy shot may result. Swing cutters should be drilled to be ready to shoot as soon as they receive the basketball. If the cut is made properly, many good shots will occur if this key point is stressed.

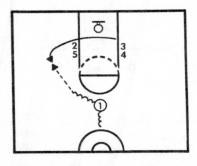

Diagram 4-8.

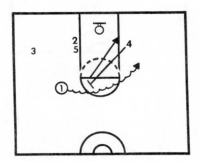

Diagram 4-9.

The No. 3 Play. The second play in the Stack Series is called our number three play. The point man calls "Stack" to indicate the initial formation. Then, 1 calls the number "three." This indicates that the 3 man will be the cutter behind the double screen being set by 2 and 5. 1 may pass to 3 who has cut behind the double screen (Diagram 4-8). 1 should keep his dribble alive if he decides to dribble back to the off side for the next option in the series.

Diagram 4-9 shows the second option in the sequence, called the "Weak-side Pick and Roll Option." This is a continuation of the five-play sequence mentioned at the start of this chapter. 1, who optioned not to pass to 3 on the first option off the double screen, dribbles back to the off side and 4 moves into the high post area at the free-throw line to set a stationary screen for 1. 1 should look for the jump shot or the drive as soon as he dribbles by the screen by 4. 4 will roll out to the basket after screening for 1. To guard against the offensive charging foul on the roll out, 4 rolls to the outside of the lane as shown in Diagram 4-9. A good defensive team will sag off and help with the two defensive men covering 2 and 5, so the direction of the roll out should be altered to avoid this additional support.

Rather than run the Pick and Roll play to the off side, the coach may prefer to create the isolation of a good one-on-one man shown in Diagram

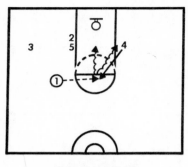

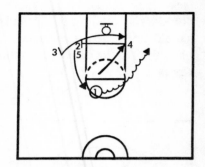

Diagram 4-10.   Diagram 4-11.

4-10 in the weak-side option for 4. This play may be pre-arranged or the point man 1 may pass to 4 and decide not to cut around or dribble around 4 as he did in the Pick and Roll option previously described.

If 4 is being heavily overplayed, he may reverse cut to the basket and receive a pass from 1. This has been an effective play against pressure man-to-man defense. There will be very little help, none on the weak side, so 4 will have one-half of the offensive court in which to operate one-on-one. We like to get our quickest post man in the 4 spot for the isolation option. The No. 3 play has been used as a decoy play just to set up the isolation option to 4.

Diagram 4-11 illustrates the Baseline Cutter option off play No. 3. 1 dribbles back to the weak side, 4 has rolled out to the ball and just as 1 picks up his dribble, 2 cuts to the free-throw line, 4 moves on across the lane to set a double screen with 5 for 3. 3 sets up his cut by faking away from the direction of his intended cut. 3 cuts along the baseline behind the double screen set by 4 and 5. 1 may pass to 3 if the cutter is open, or continue the final play in the sequence—the Double Swing shown in Diagram 4-12.

If 3 does not receive the pass from 1, the pass is made to 2 at the free-throw line. 1 will move in to screen for 3. 3 and 4 will run the Swing cut from behind their respective screeners. 5 and 1. 2 hits the open cutter who takes the quick jump shot, if open (Diagram 4-12).

The No. 4 Play. The number Four play is designed to set a double screen play for post man 4. To initiate the play, 1 calls "4." Players 2 and 5 set a double screen on the left side of the free-throw lane. 4 cuts around the double screen on the baseline side. If 4 is open, he may receive a pass from 1 for the jump shot (Diagram 4-13). Remember, 1 must keep his

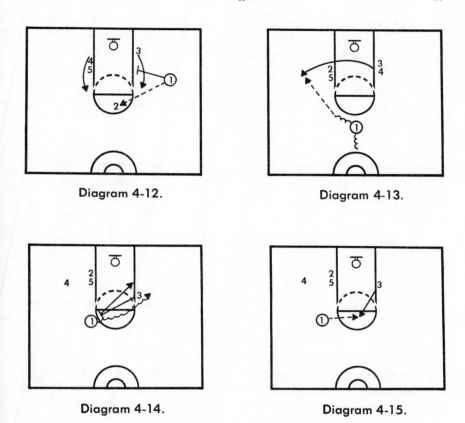

Diagram 4-12.

Diagram 4-13.

Diagram 4-14.

Diagram 4-15.

dribble going so he can keep the weak-side Pick and Roll option alive. 1 must make the decision to pass to 4 or reverse the ball to the weak side for the weak-side options.

The weak-side Pick and Roll option is shown in Diagram 4-14. 1, who decided not to pass to 4 on the first option, dribbles around a screen being set by the off-side man 3. 1 looks for the jump shot or passes to the roll-out man, 3. 3, the wing guard, must use the same rule for rolling out as we described for the post men 4 and 5, to prevent the player control foul.

If we decide to use the No. 4 play to create an isolation situation for the 3 man, 1 will pass to 3 instead of using the dribble pick-and-roll play. After receiving the pass from 1, 3 pivots to face his defensive man and the basket. By using various step fakes, 3 may set up the jump shot or drive, depending on the defensive man's reaction to the offensive fakes (Diagram 4-15).

The next progression in the series is the Baseline Cutter option shown in Diagram 4-16. This play is keyed by the roll-out play being terminated unsuccessfully. 1 retains the ball. 3 moves across the line to set the double screen with 5. 2 cuts to the free-throw line. 4 cuts behind the double screen by 3 and 5 to the basket for a possible return pass from 1. Shooting options may occur with the pass to 4 or the pass to 2 at the free-throw line.

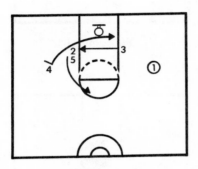

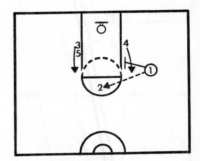

Diagram 4-16.   Diagram 4-17.

The final play in the sequence of options is the Double Swing option shown in Diagram 4-17. 1 passes the ball back to 2 at the free-throw line. 3 will cut around 5, looking for a pass from 2. On the right side of the court, 1, after passing to 2, screens for 4 who swing-cuts around the screen for a possible pass from 2. This second swing cut is slightly delayed because 1 has to pass before making his screen. This delay gives 3 and 5 time to run the Swing option on the left side.

A slight variation of the Double Swing option is shown in Diagram 4-18. 3, instead of cutting around 5, cuts to a wider position on the wing. 2 then passes to 3, who looks inside to 5 for a post pass. We have found this variation to be an excellent way to get the ball to the post men on the inside.

The No. 5 Play. The number Five Play is designed to provide a double screen option for the post man 5. To begin the No. 5 play, the point man 1 calls "Five." Post man 5 cuts behind a double screen being set by 3 and 4 on the right side of the free-throw lane. If 5 is open for a shot, 1 hits him with a quick pass (Diagram 4-19). If he does not appear to be open, 1 continues his dribble and runs the next option in the sequence of plays.

Diagram 4-20 shows the next option, the Weak-side Pick and Roll

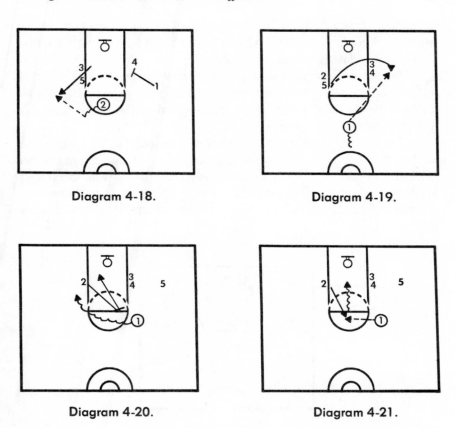

Diagram 4-18.

Diagram 4-19.

Diagram 4-20.

Diagram 4-21.

play. 2 cuts to the free-throw line to set a screen on 1's defensive man. 1 immediately looks for the good jump shot or the chance to drive all the way to the basket for the lay-up. 2 rolls out to the basket and may receive a pass from 1. 2 may also establish a low post position and receive a pass from 1. This is an excellent chance to take advantage of a defensive mismatch on 2 or if our man is much taller than 2. This posting and guard maneuver is not used as much as it should be by most coaches and a coach would be wise to consider this plan for attacking the opponent's defenses.

Diagram 4-21 illustrates how we create the isolation option for wing guard 2. If we have decided to try to create the isolation rather than use the previously described pick-and-roll play, 1 will pass to 2 rather than use his screen. It is necessary for the players to know if we are going to use the isolation play because 2's cut will be slightly different than if he were screening. 2 must delay his cut to the ball until he sees 1 is ready to make a move back to the weak side. Also, 2 must be prepared to cut to the ball against overplaying defensive pressure.

We have discovered that the reverse cut to the basket is highly effective if 2 is being heavily overplayed on the cut to the ball. The now famous "Alley Oop" pass play may be executed on the reverse cut with a lob pass from 1 being thrown to 2.

The Baseline Cutter option is shown in Diagram 4-22. 1 retains the ball on the weak-side pick and roll. 3, after not receiving a return pass on his roll-out or posting maneuver, cuts across the lane to set a double screen on the right side of the free-throw lane with 4. 3 cuts to the free-throw line. 5 fakes and cuts along the baseline side of the screens for a possible pass from 1.

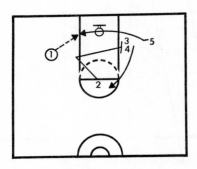

Diagram 4-22.

Occasionally, we will instruct the baseline cutter to make his cut over the top of the double screen rather than on the baseline side. This tactic will help counter overplaying techniques by the defense and will also aid in setting up the Double Swing option.

The Double Swing option is keyed with the pass from 1 to 3 at the free-throw line. 2 cuts around 4 for a possible pass from 3. 1 moves in to set a screen for 5 who cuts around the screen for a possible pass from 3 (Diagram 4-23). The swing cuts may be flared out as described in Diagram 4-18 to take advantage of inside defensive mis-matches. We strongly advocate the posting maneuver because of the high-percentage area where the shot may occur and the frequency with which defensive fouls are called on the maneuver.

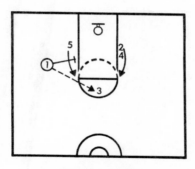

Diagram 4-23.

Many coaches will not use the inside options if they do not have big post men. For several years, I fell into this category, but through experimentation of the inside game in practice during the off season, I became convinced the ball should go inside as often as possible.

The two post men on our 1974-75 team were only 6′ 1″ and 6′ 3″, but both players shot over 53 percent from the field while compiling scoring averages of 12.5 and 15.5 points per game. These two men out-rebounded much taller teams all season because of their mobility underneath the basket.

Another factor to consider in using the inside posting maneuvers is the high-percentage area in which all shots are taken. Why let an offensive man come down and gun the ball from a low-percentage area outside the free-throw line when we can get the high-percentage shot in the 48 percent to 60 percent area?

The No. 1 Play. The final option in the Stack Series is called the Number One Play. The reason we saved this play until last is that it was the final play we installed in the series, because we wanted to have our point man handling the basketball most of the time as shown in the other diagrams in this chapter.

Diagram 4-24 shows the No. 1 Play. The option is keyed by 1, who calls the play "One." We have designated 2 as the ball handler in this sequence. However, if the second best ball handler is 3, he may cut to the ball and be the ball handler.

1 passes to 2 and cuts down the lane on the Give and Go play. 2 dribbles toward the right side of the court and may pass to 1 who has cut behind the double screen being set by 3 and 4 on the right side of the

Diagram 4-24.

free-throw lane. If 1 is open, he receives the pass from 2 and looks for the jump shot behind the double screen. 2 is also instructed to keep the dribble going if he sees 1 not open.

The Weak-side Pick and Roll option is the second play 2 has available if the pass is not made to 1. Diagram 4-25 shows this play. 5, the off-side man, cuts to the free-throw line to set a screen on 2's defensive man. 2 may drive to the left, looking for the jump shot or the drive all the way to the basket. 5, after screening for 2, rolls out to the basket for a possible pass from 2 or continues on through to the left side and establishes a low post position. He may again receive a pass from 2 and take his defensive man one-on-one in the pivot position.

Diagram 4-25.

If the Isolation option has been designated instead of the Pick and Roll option, or if 2 picked up his dribble, 5 will cut to meet a pass from 2 and will run the Isolation option shown in Diagram 4-26.

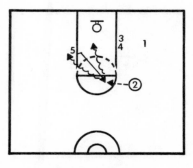

Diagram 4-26.

The Pick and Roll option may also be run off the pass from 2 to 5.

The Isolation option for 5 begins with the cut by 5 to the free-throw line. He receives a pass from 2 and pivots to face the basket or wheels back to drive to the basket. 5 drives to the basket or shoots, depending on the amount and kind of defensive pressure he faces (Diagram 4-26).

The "Alley Oop" pass and reverse play may be run if 5 is being overplayed. 5 reverses to the basket and 2 lobs the ball over the defensive man's head for the layup.

The Baseline Cutter play is shown in Diagram 4-27. 2 dribbles back to the left side. 5 screens and rolls to the basket. If 5 does not receive a pass from 2, he moves across the free-throw lane and sets a double screen with 4 on the right side of the free-throw lane. 3 cuts to the free-throw line and 1 cuts along the baseline behind the double screen by 5 and 4 to the basket. 2 may pass to 1, if he is open, or to 3 at the free-throw line to run the Double Swing option.

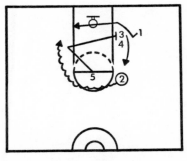

Diagram 4-27.

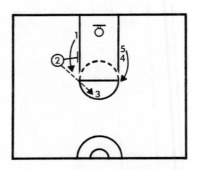

Diagram 4-28.

Diagram 4-28 illustrates how the Double Swing is run. 2 passes the ball outside to 3 at the free-throw line. 5 cuts around the screen by 4 for a possible pass from 3. 2, after passing to 3, moves in to set a screen for 1 on the left side of the free-throw lane. 1 cuts around the screen by 2 for a possible pass from 3.

The Stack Series presented in this chapter is highly adaptable to all kinds of personnel. Coaches may select one or all of the various options described to add to their offensive system. We think many high-percentage shots may result in the proper execution of the Five Basic Plays and the variety of methods shown to run these plays, and we hope that coaches using this series for the first time will have the same success with the series as we have.

CHAPTER 5

Adapting the Red Cat Shuffle
Series to the 1-2-2

The Red Cat Shuffle Series grew out of several immediate needs I faced when moving to Oak Ridge. The squad I inherited had graduated eight of the top 12 players, plus all five starters. The player with the highest point-per-game average returning had a 3.1 average, and he decided to forgo his senior year of eligibility in order to work.

After conducting spring tryouts from the student body, we found ourselves with an inexperienced squad composed of three returning players with very limited experience, one transfer (the coach's son), two players from a church league, and several upcoming players from the junior varsity squad.

To install a complete offensive and defensive system takes several months at best. This time was not available, so I decided to put in a simple pattern based on shuffle principles, and to add to the system as the season progressed. The basic pattern I obtained from Coach Steve Moore, Head Basketball Coach at Oak Hills High School in Cincinnati, Ohio. I adapted the offense to the 1-2-2, using several different alignments which are shown later in this chapter.

ADVANTAGES OF THE RED CAT SHUFFLE

The Red Cat Shuffle presents a series of maneuvers which allowed us an offense with these advantages.

Effective in Tempo Control

The Red Cat Shuffle series can be easily adapted to both the fast or slow tempo, depending on the coach's preference. We have used this series as a quick-hitting offense and as a delay game, taking only lay-ups or high-percentage shots. Our current philosophy about running a delay game (withholding the ball late in the game) is to continue trying to score on high-percentage shots as opposed to just holding the ball and hoping the opponents will foul. Our basic rule is to take only the good shots, preferably an unmolested lay-up. If the good shot is not obtained, we continue the shuffle pattern.

High-Percentage Shots

One of the unique features of this series is that no shot has to be taken beyond the 15-foot range. This factor has increased our team's field goal shooting percentage from close to 40 percent to close to 50 percent. Many power lay-ups and close-to-the-basket jump shots are available with proper execution.

Good Continuity

Movement on offense, with or without the ball, is essential to obtain maximum offensive efficiency. The Red Cat Shuffle affords constant team movement. This continuity insures the necessary player movement which will require constant defensive adjustments by the opponents. Counter options will be shown to insure a smooth continuity regardless of the type of defensive pressure being faced.

Balanced Attack

Few teams have a super star every year and, as a result, most coaches have to rely on all five men to do the bulk of their scoring. The shuffle-type offense presents each player good scoring opportunities. For teams who rely on two or three players to do most of their scoring, this offense is not recommended, but the series does allow for individual offensive maneuvering for an outstanding player at several positions in the continuity. For example, if a team has a good driving guard or forward, he may be placed in the 5 position in the pattern. After the initial entry pass and screen by 5, he rotates to the ball at the free-throw line. After receiving the ball, he may drive prior to the baseline screen and post cut. Often, we would hold the baseline cut until the one-on-one option had taken place.

The first year we used the Red Cat Shuffle, three starters averaged in double figures while the other two men averaged eight and nine points apiece. This feature aids in developing team morale since every player gets good chances to score and different players share in high point honors. The players get recognition in the newspapers and on the radio broadcasts. This public recognition helps in keeping them motivated.

Excellent Offense for Small Teams

Because of the constant movement of players, the offense helps offset any height advantage the opponents may have. Big men must move to a variety of spots on the floor in order to cover their men. Many times our center has rotated to the free-throw line, losing his defensive man completely, for wide-open jump shots.

Another factor in facing a larger team to be considered is that of trying to rebound. This offensive series takes the opponent's center to areas where he usually does not go, thus our smaller players may beat them to the board. We have out-rebounded many larger teams because of this factor.

Develops Good Ball Handling

One of the side benefits of this offensive series is the development of good, overall, team ball handling. All five men must handle the basketball and over a period of a few weeks the ball-handling skills progress rapidly.

We have used the Red Cat Shuffle and the Wheel series as ball-handling drills. Both series are excellent for this purpose.

Variety of Screening Options

As many teams in our area went to the Auburn Shuffle, the Wheel and other offenses using the basic off-side shuffle cuts, we wanted an offense that used these same cuts, but from different angles. This series provides many screening possibilities and incorporates the best features of the two offenses mentioned above.

We have used this series as a part of our man-to-man attack along with the Wildcat Rotation with outstanding results.

Drives Teams out of Man-to-Man Defenses

Because of the many screen adjustments that must be made, we have forced many teams to abandon their basic man-to-man defense and go to some form of zone defense. It is almost impossible to stop this series without switching, and many defensive mistakes occur when switching occurs, thus enabling the offense to take immediate advantage of these errors. By forcing man-to-man defensive teams out of their basic defense, we are usually able to tear apart their secondary defenses.

DIFFERENT ALIGNMENTS FOR THE SERIES

All of our offensive patterns begin with the same 1-2-2 alignment. However, to make our opponents think we are doing something different, we will show several versions of the 1-2-2 formation.

The first variation from the standard 1-2-2 is called "Tight and High."

The main difference in this alignment is in the placement of the wing guards. Instead of setting up midway between the sidelines and the free-throw lane, 2 and 3 set up just outside the free-throw lane in the high side post positions. The main advantage of this alignment is that 2 and 3 are closer to the basket and the pass they must make after receiving the ball is much shorter than from the wider 1-2-2 formation. It is also easier for them to step out to meet the ball being passed to them by 1. The formation also gives 2 and 3 more room to the outside to get open for the pass without a possible defensive interception (Diagram 5-1).

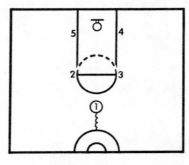

Diagram 5-1.

A second variation is the "Double Stack" alignment. Diagram 5-2 shows our Double Stack A. The wing guards, 2 and 3, set up just in front of the post men 4 and 5. This is used when we are combining the Red Cat Shuffle series with the Stack series. One series actually acts as a decoy for the other.

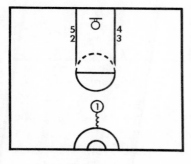

Diagram 5-2.

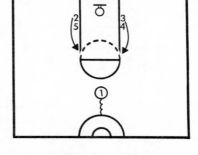

Diagram 5-3.

Diagram 5-3 shows our Double Stack B formation. Wing guards 2 and 3 set up behind the two post men 4 and 5. This alignment presents more of a defensive problem for the opponents than Double Stack A because the guards have to get around our post man and his defensive post in order to get to his man, and he must fight harder to go over the top of a screen set by the post men. If a switch occurs to prevent the entry pass, our opponent's center will have to cover outside which gives our post man a mismatch inside. If this occurs, our post man calls for the ball, steps in the lane to receive a pass from 1, and we try to overpower the defensive man who switched to cover inside.

RELEASE MOVES

To counter extreme defensive pressure when facing teams with much quicker personnel, we added a number of moves called "Release Moves" in order to complete the entry pass more easily. The first release move we simply name "Release."

The point man, upon seeing tight man-to-man pressure on the wing guards, calls "Release." Wing guards 2 and 3 go pick the respective

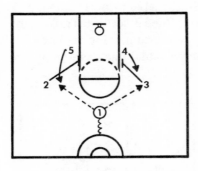

Diagram 5-4.

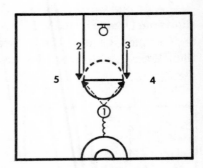

Diagram 5-5.

opponent's defensive post men. 4 and 5 "pop out" to the wings and get the entry pass (Diagram 5-4). We then go into the basic continuity after 1 passed the ball to one of the two men who popped out. If switches occurred, the two wing men would step up the outside of the lane and get a pass from 1 (Diagram 5-5).

If the opponents switched the guards on our post men, this left our wing guards being covered by our slower opponent's big men. By stepping up the lane, the wing men could easily get open to begin the offense.

The Release moves may be restricted to one side or the other as shown in Diagrams 5-6 and 5-7. In Diagram 5-6, the point man calls "Release Right." Wing guard 3 goes down and sets a screen on 4's defensive man. 4 fakes into the lane and pops out to the wing position for the entry pass from 1.

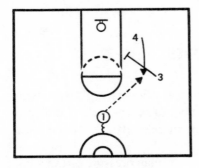

Diagram 5-6.

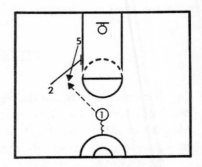

Diagram 5-7.

In Diagram 5-7, the point man calls "Release Left." Wing guard 2 goes down and sets a screen on 5's defensive man. 5 fakes into the lane and pops out to the left wing position for the entry pass from 1.

Occasionally, we call the "X" release. This is a rather unorthodox move, but does give additional variety when we are using the Red Cat Shuffle series as our only offense against the man-to-man defense. In this release move, the point man calls "X." Wing men 2 and 3 each cut across the lane to the opposite side to become post men. At the same time, post men 4 and 5 cut across the lane to the high side post positions. The cuts resemble an X, thus the name "X" for his maneuver (Diagram 5-8).

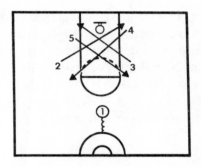

Diagram 5-8.

To confuse the defense further, the point man may call any of the other previously described release moves. Seldom does a point man use all of the release moves described, but two or three should be incorporated into the offensive plans to give the offensive series a wider variety of offensive maneuvers with which the defense must cope.

THE RED CAT SHUFFLE—BASIC ROTATION

The basic rotation is shown in Diagrams 5-9 through 5-19. All of the diagrams will begin from the standard 1-2-2 alignment.

Diagram 5-9 shows the initial pass and cuts. 1 passes to the wing guard 3 and cuts outside. Occasionally, 3 will give the ball back if 1 is a good outside jump shooter. Also, the defensive man guarding 1 may try to double-team 3. If this happens, we tell 1 to call for the ball. He usually will

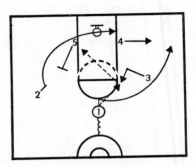

Diagram 5-9.

get a clear jump shot. This maneuver also creates an overload or triangle on the strong side against zone defenses. As soon as the pass is made to 3, 5 sets a stationary screen on 2's defensive man. 2, using the fake-right-go-left maneuver, cuts to the basket for a possible pass from 3. Our team has gotten as many as eight lay-ups in a game from this backdoor cut.

2 has the option to go back door or over the top of the screen (Diagram 5-10). This second cut will free 5 if the opponents are not switching.

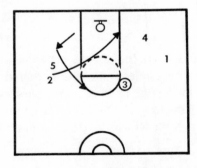

Diagram 5-10.

To complete the action on the initial entry pass, 4 moves out about three steps, faking a cut to the corner to get the ball, in order to give 2 room to set a legal screen just outside the free-throw lane area. By moving out, 4's defensive man must play him tighter. If not covered, 3 may pass quickly down to 4 for the quick jump shot.

Thus 3, upon receiving the ball, may pass to 1, 2 under the basket (preferred pass), 4 on the baseline (only if 3 is sure 4 has a shot), or to 5 cutting into the high post area after having screened for 2 on the backdoor or shuffle cut.

Phase two of the basic rotation occurs if 3 passes to 5. Diagram 5-11 shows a continuation of the pattern. After receiving the pass from 3, 5 may shoot if open, drive to the basket, or pass to 4 who has cut along the baseline behind a screen set by 2 (the first cutter through). 4 should set up his cut by faking a cut toward 3. Most of the time we prefer 4 to cut on the baseline side of 2, but occasionally he may cut over the top or on the free-throw line side of the screen.

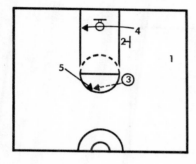

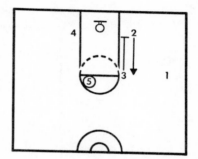

Diagram 5-11.   Diagram 5-12.

Step three occurs after 3 has passed to 5. 3 picks down the lane for 2 who cuts to the spot vacated by 3. 2 should fake toward the basket to set up the cut off the screen (Diagram 5-12). If 2 receives the pass from 5, he should immediately look for the jump shot. After passing to 2, 5 picks down for 4 who cuts to the high side post position (Diagram 5-13).

If 2 does not have the shot, he passes to 4 and cuts outside (Diagram 5-14). This move begins the rotation all over again, only to the left side. After the pass to 4 is made and 2 cuts outside, 3 sets a stationary screen on 1 who cuts along the baseline to the basket. He has the same options on the cut as 2 did on the initial pass. (See Diagram 5-9.) 4 looks inside as soon as he gets the ball for cutter 1.

After screening for 1, 3 cuts to the high post area to get a pass from 4. Upon receiving this pass, 3 may shoot if open, drive, or pass to 5 who has cut behind the screen set by cutter 1 who did not receive the ball on the previous cut (Diagram 5-15).

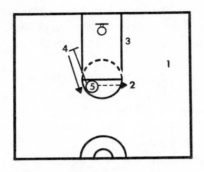

Diagram 5-13.

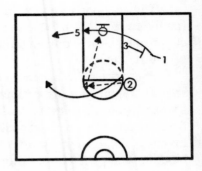

Diagram 5-14.

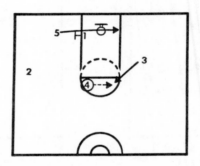

Diagram 5-15.

Special Freeze the Baseline Cutter Rule

If we are able to get the isolated driving option when the ball is passed to the high post area (as in Diagrams 5-11 and 5-15), we may use what we call the "Freeze the Baseline Cutter Rule." We delay the cut until the man with the ball at the high post spot does his own thing with the ball—shoot or drive. We have had a lot of success with this option against pressure defenses trying to play between the man and the ball.

While this same freeze rule is in effect, we will operate our quick backdoor cut (Diagram 5-16). If 3 is being denied the ball by a tough defensive man, he fakes hard to the ball, pushes off on his outside foot, and reverses to the basket. This option is especially effective when our post men, who are quick, make this cut. One or two baskets on the reverse

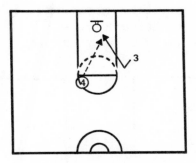

Diagram 5-16.

cut will really open up the high post pass. The opposing coach usually jumps all over his players for allowing the reverse cut basket and the players are going to make sure it doesn't happen again, thus opening up the original intent, to get the ball to the cutter in the high post area.

4 must be able to read the defense in order to make the reverse successful. He must pass to the cutter (3 in this case) at the precise moment 3 has beaten his man. Do not force the pass. 3, if not open, may re-cut to the ball and the freeze rule is out and the pattern continues.

Pressure defenses trying to deny the pass across the top of the free throw area are very vulnerable to this option. The coach using this series should drill on the reverse cut option to increase the success obtained from the basic Red Cat Shuffle.

The continuity is shown in Diagram 5-17. After passing to 3, 4 picks down for 1, who cuts to the high post area. 3 passes the ball to 1 who

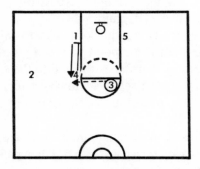

Diagram 5-17.

immediately looks for the shot. After passing to 1, 3 also picks down for 5, who cuts to the high post area on the right side. If 1 does not have the shot, he passes to 5 who may shoot (Diagram 5-18).

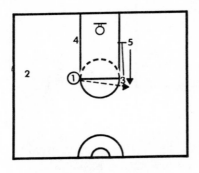

Diagram 5-18.

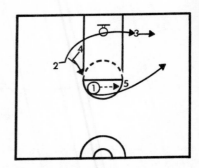

Diagram 5-19.

After passing to 5, 1 cuts outside. 4 screens for 2, who cuts to the basket for a possible pass from 5 (Diagram 5-19). This is the beginning of the basic pattern to the right side. Seldom will a team have to go through two complete rotations in order to get a good shot. It has been our experience that a good shot will usually develop on the second, third or fourth pass.

Supplementary Entries

Two additional methods of entry into the basic Red Cat Series that are extremely useful are the Dribble Entry by the point man (Diagram 5-20) and the Post Entry (Diagram 5-24).

The Dribble Entry is the quickest way to initiate the offensive pattern and may be used if the point man can get the ball to the high side post position easily. 1 dribbles the ball to the entry position. As 1 approaches the entry spot, 5 sets a stationary screen on 2, who cuts to the basket. 1 hits 2 for a pass if he is open or passes to 5 to continue the rotation (Diagram 5-20).

If 1 passes to 5 as shown in Diagram 5-21, 2 screens for 4, who cuts along the baseline looking for a pass from 5. 1 then picks down for 2, who cuts to the high post area. 5 can shoot, drive pass to 4, or pass to 2 and the Red Cat Shuffle rotation continues.

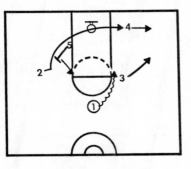

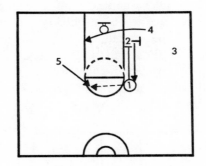

Diagram 5-20.   Diagram 5-21.

The Dribble Entry to the left side is shown in Diagram 5-22. 1 dribbles to the entry position at the left side of the free-throw lane. As he reaches that spot, 4 sets a stationary screen on 3, who cuts to the basket. 1 may pass to 3 if he is open on the initial cut, or pass to 4. (See Diagram 5-23.)

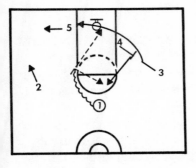

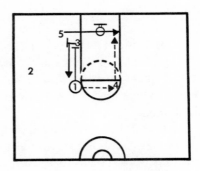

Diagram 5-22.   Diagram 5-23.

If 1 passes to 4 who has cut to the high post area after screening for 3, he picks down for 3 who has been screening for 5. 5 cuts along the baseline for a possible pass from 4. 4 has the option to shoot, drive, pass to 5 on the baseline or pass to the man cutting up to the high post spot opposite him (3). After passing, 4 picks down to continue the rotation (Diagram 5-23).

The two Dribble Entries are simple, but develop quickly and further add to the complexity of the whole offensive system for the opponents who have to adjust quickly, or lose.

The straight Post Entry Method is handled in two ways. The first is called "Post Entry Right." The point man may call this entry or it may be predetermined by the coach at any time. In Diagram 5-24, 4 cuts hard to the ball after faking to his right. 1 passes to 4 and cuts outside. 5 screens for 2 who cuts to the basket. 3 replaces 4 on the baseline for the next option.

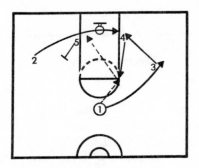

Diagram 5-24.

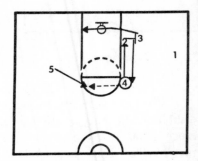

Diagram 5-25.

If 4 did not hit the cutter 2, he passes to 5 who has cut to the high post area on the left side after screening for the original cutter 2. After passing to 5, 4 picks down for 2 who has already set a screen for 3, the baseline cutter (Diagram 5-25). Continue the Basic Rotation as previously diagrammed.

Post Entry Left is called by the point man or is predetermined in the game plan. 5 cuts hard to the ball to receive a pass from 1, who then cuts to the outside. 4 screens for 3 who cuts to the basket (Diagram 5-26). 5 may hit 3 on the cut or pass to 4 who has moved to the post area (Diagram 5-27). If 5 passes to 4, he then picks down for 3 who has already set a screen on 2, the baseline cutter. The Post Entries are also quick hitting and are easy to learn.

OFFENSIVE REBOUND AND SAFETY ASSIGNMENTS

In Diagrams 5-28 through 5-42, compare with the numbered diagram listed by each explanation of the rebounding and defensive assignment.

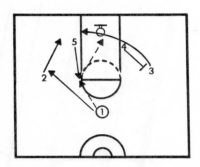

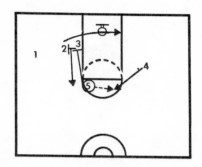

Diagram 5-26.   Diagram 5-27.

On a shot by 2, 3 and 4 take the off-side and front rebounding spot. 2 rebounds on the ball side as does 5. 1 rotates out to become the safety man (Diagram 5-28). If we are playing an opponent who likes to fast break, 3 may be assigned to take the outlet man.

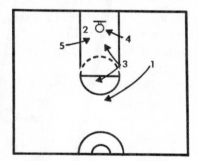

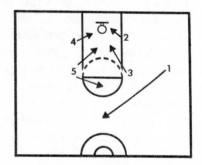

Diagram 5-28.   Diagram 5-29.
(See Offensive Diagram 5-9.)   (See Offensive Diagram 5-12).

We will send four men to the offensive boards until we get hurt a few times. The main responsibility of the safety man is to prevent anyone from getting behind him. On a shot by 5 or 4, 2 and 3 take the off-side spots with 4 and 5 rebounding from the ball side (Diagram 5-29).

5 may be assigned outlet pass duties. With 2 shooting, 4 and 5 rebound in the off-side and front position; 3 the ball side, 2 ball-side front or outlet responsibilities, and 1 the safety position (Diagram 5-30). Usually, we want 1 to rotate to the safety position because of his speed and

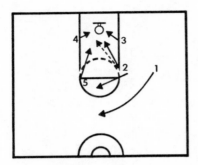

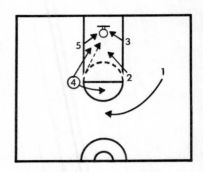

Diagram 5-30.
(See Offensive Diagram 5-13.)

Diagram 5-31.
(See Offensive Diagram 5-14.)

quickness. Also, the other four men are usually bigger and probably better rebounders.

Diagram 5-31 shows the rebounding and safety pattern on a shot by 4. 2 and 3 take the off-side and front positions, with 5 rebounding the ball-side spot. 4 follows shot or rotates to the assigned rebound spot.

On a shot by 3 or 5, 1 takes the off-side low position since he is the closest man to the basket. 4 rebounds the front spot. 5 fills the low spot on the ball side while 3 either crashes the boards or takes the outlet man. 2 rotates to the safety position (Diagram 5-32).

With 1 shooting (Diagram 5-33), 5 crashes the boards on the off-side low position, 3 fills the off-side front position and 4 crashes low on the ball side. 1 may follow his shot or go to the outlet man to stop the quick break by the opponents. 2 rotates to the safety position.

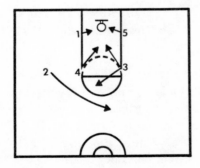

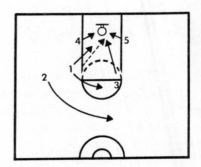

Diagram 5-32.
(See Offensive Diagram 5-15.)

Diagram 5-33.
(See Offensive Diagram 5-18.)

In Diagram 5-34, 4 shoots. Rebounding the off-side positions are 2 in the low spot, 5 in the front position, and 3 fills the low ball-side spot, 4 can follow his shot or go to the outlet man. 1 becomes the safety man.

On a shot by 2, 2 and 4 rebound on the ball side, 5 crashes the off side. 1 can follow or go to the outlet man. Generally, the 1 man does not go to the boards unless he is in one of the low positions or if he shoots. 3 becomes the safety man (Diagram 5-35).

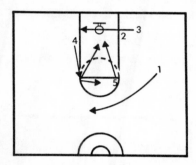

Diagram 5-34.
(See Offensive Diagram 5-19.)

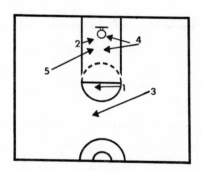

Diagram 5-35.
(See Diagram 5-20, Dribble Entry.

2 shoots. 4 and 5 move to fill the off-side low and front positions. 1, being closest to the basket on the ball side. 2 can crash or go to the outlet position. 3 rotates to the defensive safety position (Diagram 5-36).

4 shoots. 3 and 1 fill the off-side low and front positions. 5, after his

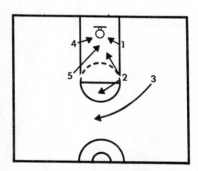

Diagram 5-36.
(See Diagram 5-21,
Dribble Entry, Right.)

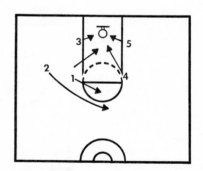

Diagram 5-37.
(See Diagram 5-22,
Dribble Entry Left.)

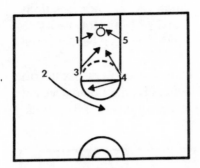

Diagram 5-38.
(See Diagram 5-23,
Dribble Entry Left.)

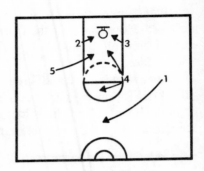

Diagram 5-39.
(See Diagram 5-24, Post Entry.)

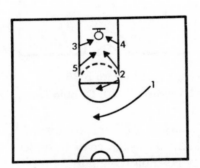

Diagram 5-40.
(See Diagram 5-25, Post Entry.)

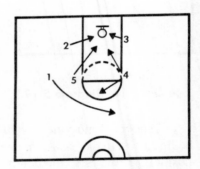

Diagram 5-41.
(See Diagram 5-26, Post Entry.)

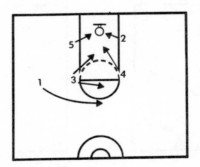

Diagram 5-42.
(See Diagram 5-27, Post Entry.)

initial cut, will be in a position to rebound on the ball side. 4 can follow his shot or check the outlet pass. 2 rotates to the defensive safety position (Diagram 5-37).

4 shoots. 1 and 3 fill the off-side low and front spots. 5 rebounds low on the ball side. 4 may follow or check the outlet pass. 2 rotates to the defensive safety position (Diagram 5-38).

4 shoots. 2 and 5 move to fill the off-side low and front positions. 3 crashes low on ball side. 4 can follow or go to the possible outlet pass. 1 rotates to the defensive safety position (Diagram 5-39).

2 shoots. 3 and 5 fill the off-side low and front positions. 4 crashes low on ball side. 2 may follow or go to the outlet man. 1 rotates to defensive safety spot (Diagram 5-40).

Shot by 3 or 4. 2 and 5 crash in the off-side low and front positions. 4 can crash or go to the outlet pass. 1 becomes the defensive safety (Diagram 5-41).

Shot by 3. 2 and 4 fill the off-side low and front spots. 3 can follow or go to the outlet pass. 1 rotates to the safety position (Diagram 5-42).

Much emphasis has been placed on offensive rebounding. Many teams take this important aspect too lightly. Offensive rebounding is a vital part of the 1-2-2 offensive system and is one of the factors in developing winning teams.

Some coaches may be wary of sending four men to the offensive board. In these cases, an optional rule is to send the second man on the ball side to a lateral position even with the safety man. This optional rule can strengthen a team against an opponent's possible fast break.

CHAPTER **6**

Combining Special Plays
with the 1-2-2 Offense

EVALUATION OF PERSONNEL

The first step in the planning of an offensive system is the evaluation of the returning personnel. In our school we have grades 10 through 12 and have two teams, a junior varsity (composed only of sophomores) and a varsity team (composed of juniors and seniors and any sophomores who excel enough to start). We use sophomores on the varsity only as a last resort.

At the completion of a basketball season, we schedule evaluation conferences with each returning player. These individual conferences include an evaluation in 11 areas, using the Evaluation Chart shown on the following page.

SPRING PRACTICE

The next step is to compile a list of team strengths and weaknesses. The team we began building this season included two returning starters, one part-time starter, and three other players who participated rather sparingly. Up from the junior varsity team we had 12 candidates with only junior varsity experience. From the general tryout sessions we hold in the spring, three other players were added to the spring practice group.

With this group, we have two to three weeks of spring basketball

BASKETBALL EVALUATION FORM

NAME OF PLAYER_____

KEY TO RATINGS: 1-Outstanding; 2-Above Average; 3-Average; 4-Below
                  Average

CHARACTERISTICS RATED	RATING	COMMENTS
1. SIZE		
2. SPEED-QUICKNESS		
3. ATTITUDE		
4. LEADERSHIP OBSERVED		
5. DEFENSIVE ABILITY		
6. ACADEMIC ABILITY		
7. BALL HANDLING ABILITY		
8. REBOUNDING ABILITY		
9. JUMPING ABILITY		
10. SCORING ABILITY		
11. ABILITY TO RESPOND TO INSTRUCTION		

POSITION PLAYED:

RANKING AT POSITION:

OVERALL SQUAD RANKING:

NAMES OF PLAYERS RANKED ABOVE YOUR SON:

ADDITIONAL COMMENTS BY COACH MAKING EVALUATION:_____

_____

_____

_____

NAME OF COACH MAKING EVALUATIONS

practice. The practice sessions run daily for approximately two hours each. The first hour is devoted to individual fundamentals (both offensive and defensive skills included). The second hour is devoted to various types of scrimmaging, one-on-one, two-on-two, three-on-three and five-on-five full court.

After the first week, players are rated at the positions for which they are trying out and this list is posted. We allow challenges in the spring. If a player feels he is better than someone above him on the rating list, he requests the right to challenge the player in one-on-one competition. If he wins, he moves up the list. It should be noted that, occasionally, players are not as good in one-on-one competition as they might be in team play and the coach should not use the one-on-one method as the sole basis for selection. This fact should be pointed out to the players, or some misunderstandings could occur.

All players are urged to discuss their individual ratings with the coach if they are unhappy about them or want to know why they were rated in a particular position. The coach should be completely open and straightforward in answering these questions. The player may not agree, but at least he knows how and why the coach feels the way he does. The coach should also use these sessions to inform the players as to how they can improve—give specific workout suggestions.

During spring practice we try to scrimmage other teams in our immediate area. Usually, we will play two games of about seven to eight quarters each. By doing this we get to see all of the players in game-like conditions.

At the conclusion of spring practice, a list of ratings is published and given to each player. Also, the coaches compile a list of team strengths and weaknesses and begin planning for the next season.

From our evaluation of spring practice, my assistant and I compile a list of team strengths and weaknesses. An example of our list includes the following:

Team Strengths

1. Excellent shooting, wing guards;
2. Above average jumping ability;
3. Average speed and quickness at guard with excellent speed and quickness at the post positions; and
4. Adequate depth at each position.

Team Weaknesses

1. Lack of height at the post positions;
2. Inexperienced point men;
3. Man-to-man fundamentals weak;
4. Rebounding suspect due to lack of height; and
5. The top junior varsity players must be trained at new positions.

Once the team has been thoroughly evaluated, we select the offensive and defensive system that best suits our personnel. Our offensive decisions for one season are shown in the remaining pages of this chapter. An offensive Index is presented later in the chapter.

"OFFENSE '75"

The Double Left Play

The Double Left Play was included in our offensive plans because of two excellent outside-shooting wing guards. The point man 1 calls "Double Left." 1 passes to 3. Following the basic rule that the post men rotate on any pass from the point position to the wing position, 4 and 5 complete the post cuts described in Chapter 1 in the Wildcat Post Rotation options. This post rotation gives the offense additional rotation which was designed to counter much taller opponents. 1 moves down to set a double screen with 4 for the left wing guard 2. 2 must set up his defensive man by faking a baseline cut. 2 then cuts around the double screen to the free-throw line for a possible pass from 3 who has dribbled toward the free throw lane (Diagram 6-1)

3 has the following options: (1) pass to 2, (2) pass to 5 on the rollout, (3) pass to 1 on the step-in option, or (4) pass to 4 (Diagram 6-2).

Wing guard 3 may call the name option which keys the screen by 5 on 3's defensive man. 3 drives toward the middle off the screen and looks for the shot. 5 rolls out to the basket just as 3 dribbles past him (Diagram 6-3). 3 passes to 5 if he is open on the roll-out cut. One of the main advantages of running the Post Pick and Roll from this angle is the lack of defensive help behind the roll-out man.

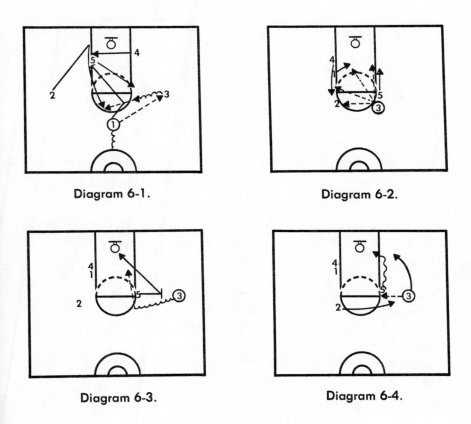

Diagram 6-1.

Diagram 6-2.

Diagram 6-3.

Diagram 6-4.

Wing guard 3 chooses to pass to 5. 3 passes and cuts quickly to the basket for a possible return pass from 5. We have gotten a quick basket on this play, especially against tight man-to-man pressure defenses. 5 also may drop-step and drive to the basket. 2 may cut around 5 for a possible pass and drive to the basket (Diagram 6-4).

The Double Right Play

The Double Right Play is a double screen play for the right wing guard. To key the play, 1 calls "Double Right". 1 then passes to the wing guard 2. 4 and 5 rotate to give post movement. 1 and 5 set a double screen off the ball for 3 who cuts toward the baseline and then cuts back to the free-throw line for a possible pass from 2 (Diagram 6-5). 2 dribbles

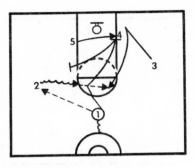

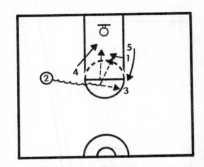

Diagram 6-5.   Diagram 6-6.

toward the middle and can pass to 3, pass to 4 on the Pick and Roll Play (Diagram 6-6) or pass to 1 on the Step-In option. 2 may also shoot after driving over the screen set by 4.

Occasionally, 1's defensive man will call a switch and pick up 3. When 1 hears the switch call or sees it occur, he steps into the lane for a possible pass from 2. This has been a good option and we have gotten several easy baskets with no one covering 1. 5 may step out behind 1 and may also receive a pass from 2.

The same Step-In option may occur after 3 receives the ball. 3 may pass to 1 or hit 5 after 1 steps into the lane.

The Blue Play

The Blue Play was inserted into the offensive system in order to counter the overplay and switching techniques employed by the opponents on the Double options.

To begin the play, 1 calls "Blue" and dribbles to a position to where the ball may be passed to wing guard 3. Post men 4 and 5 rotate, following the same Wildcat Rotation rule previously discussed when the ball is passed from the point to the wing on the Basic 1-2-2. 2 sets up his cut by faking to the baseline to make it appear he is running Double, fakes to the free-throw line and then cuts along the baseline behind a screen being set by the rotating post man 4. 3 may pass to 2 on the baseline cut if 2 is open (Diagram 6-7). The key to obtaining an easy basket is the way 2 carries out his fakes to set up the defensive man.

The second option is a screen by 5 on wing guard 3's defensive man and a drive to the basket or the free-throw lane area (Diagram 6-8). 5

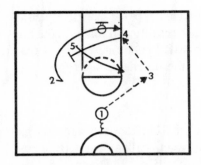

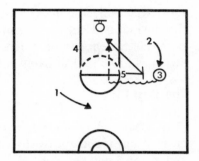

Diagram 6-7.   Diagram 6-8.

screens and then rolls out to the basket. 2, if he did not receive a pass, continues on toward the corner and rotates outside. 4 holds his low post position and if 3 penetrates, may receive a pass from 3. 1 will become the defensive safety man or may receive a pass from 3 to reset the offense.

Diagram 6-9 shows the same "Blue" play being executed to the opposite side. To start the play, 1 calls "Blue," and then dribbles to the left to pass the ball to 2. As soon as the pass is made, 4 and 5 rotate. 5 sets a screen for the off-side wing guard 3, who sets up his cut by faking to the baseline, back to the front, and then cutting behind 5's screen along the baseline to the basket. 2 may hit 3 if open or continue the pattern as shown in Diagram 6-10.

4 moves out to set a stationary screen for 2 who drives to the free-throw lane area. He should look for the shot or drive to the basket. 4 rolls out to the basket and may receive a pass from 2. 3, if he does not

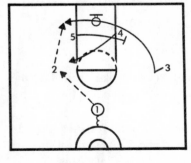

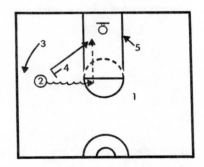

Diagram 6-9.   Diagram 6-10.

receive the ball, continues on to the corner and keeps his man occupied so that the Pick and Roll option can be run successfully. 5 remains in the low post spot to rebound or to receive a pass if 2 penetrates and 5's man switches to help. 1 remains out front as the defensive safety man.

The Post Play

The Post Play was installed to give a quick backdoor cut against tight pressure on the entry passes by 1. The point man 1 calls "Post". Both post men 4 and 5 will cut to the high side post positions. In Diagram 6-11, 1 passes to 5. As soon as 2 sees the pass to 5, he cuts hard to the basket for a possible pass from 5. In the meantime, 1, after passing to 5, fakes to his right and then cuts off 5. If 5 hands the ball off to 1, 2 continues on across the lane to clear the area for 1 to drive to the basket. If 5 keeps the ball, 1 continues on down the lane and sets a stationary screen on 2's defensive man. 2 will cut back behind the screen by 1 and look for a possible pass from 5 (Diagram 6-12). 4 remains in the low post position for rebounding purposes and 3 rotates out front to become the defensive safety man.

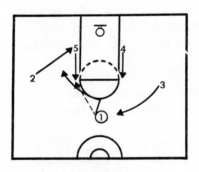
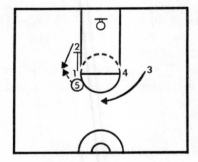

Diagram 6-11.   Diagram 6-12.

1 may establish a low post position and receive a pass from 2 for the individual offense move. This move may be used to conceal the posting the point man option.

Diagram 6-13 shows the Post option being executed on the right side of the court. 1 calls "Post." Both post men, 4 and 5, cut to the high post positions. 1 passes to 4. 3 immediately cuts to the basket, looking for a quick pass from 4. If 4 keeps the ball, he may hand off to 1, who, after

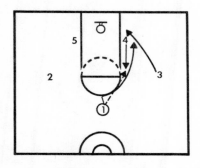

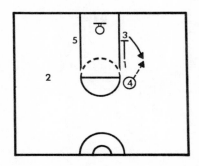

Diagram 6-13.   Diagram 6-14.

passing to 4, faked to the left and now cuts around 4 for a return pass. If 1 gets the ball, he looks for the driving lay-up or jump shot. 3 must quickly read the play and if 1 receives the ball, clear on across the lane to take the defense out of the area. If 4 does not pass to 3 or to 1 on the first cuts, 1 continues on down the right side of the free-throw lane and sets a screen for 3 (Diagram 6-14).

3 cuts back behind the screen by 1 and looks for a possible pass from 4. 3 shoots if he has the high-percentage shot or may pass inside to 1 who becomes a low post man as previously described in Diagram 6-12. 2 rotates out front to become the defensive safety man while 5 moves down to become the off-side rebounder.

The Quick Play

The Quick options were selected to take advantage of the team's speed and quickness. The point man calls "Quick" as he dribbles to the left side, looking for post man 4 who cuts toward 1. 4 should receive the pass as he approaches the free-throw line. As soon as 4 receives the ball, 3 reverses and cuts to the basket. (The reverse is made by 3 pushing off on his left foot and stepping to the basket with the right foot.) 4 passes to the cutter 3 if open. Meanwhile, 1 fakes to the left and cuts around 4. 1 may also receive a pass from 4 if the pass was not made to 3 on the reverse cut (Diagram 6-15).

Diagram 6-16 shows the same "Quick" option being executed to the right side of the court. 1 calls "Quick" as he dribbles to the right side of the court. 5, the off-side post man, cuts to the free-throw line. 1 hits 5 with a

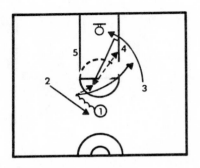

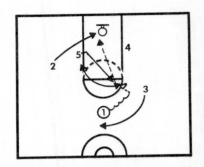

Diagram 6-15.   Diagram 6-16.

pass as 5 reaches the free-throw line. After 5 receives the pass, 2 reverses and cuts to the basket, pushing off on his right foot and stepping to the basket with the left foot. 5 may pass to the reversing cutter 2 or to 1 who has faked to the right after passing to 5, and cut around 5 for a possible return pass.

This option provides an excellent entry against tight pressure on the wing guards and against defensive wing guards who have a tendency to watch the ball and not their men. Weak-side options such as the Swing option can be added if the coach wants continuity on the play.

The Wide Play

As the season progressed, we added the Wide Play for our point man. He was an exceptionally quick, strong guard with excellent driving ability and good one-on-one offensive moves. His ability to penetrate with the ball created many problems for the defense and to take advantage of his various abilities, we installed the Wide Play.

Diagram 6-17 illustrates this simple, but effective, maneuver which became a high scoring play in our offensive system. The point man calls "Wide." The wing guards 2 and 3 reverse cut as though they were going to cut to the baseline. The post men, 4 and 5, move out to the corners. The purpose of these cuts is merely to keep their defensive men occupied so they cannot help 1's defensive man. 1 then takes his man one-on-one down the free-throw lane.

A second option was used when the defensive post men would sag to the lane area to help on 1. The offensive post men, 4 and 5, move to the basket and may receive a pass from 1.

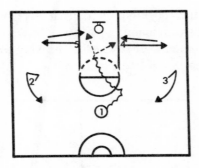

Diagram 6-17.

Our point man was left-handed and 5's defensive man would help more than 4's. As a result, 5 received many assists from 1 for power lay-ups or short baseline jump shots.

If the defensive wing men try to help, we instruct the offensive wing guards to cut to the baseline. This maneuver will make it very difficult for the defense to help and still be able to recover on our wing men. 1 may pass to the open wing man for the easy, high-percentage jump shot on the baseline.

The Wide Play is one of the most essential plays in our offensive system because of the many options created by being able to penetrate with the basketball. Coaches should strongly encourage offensive penetration with the ball from the point position if the point man can develop the necessary driving and passing skills.

The Goofy Stack

The origin of the Goofy Stack in our offensive system resulted from a good-natured bet. At a party of coaches and teachers one night, the discussion centered on the importance of certain players and their effect on the season's record. My contention was that we could take the two best players and three players from the junior varsity team and beat the best remaining varsity players.

We had several days before our next game, so I decided to experiment with a couple of plays and carry out the circumstances we had discussed. The results became known as the "Goofy Stack."

The basic premise of the offense was to stack the best two players in a tandem position on one side of the lane. The quickest man was placed behind the 5 man in the 4 position. The ball handler would be aligned in the 1 position with the two remaining players to be set in the 2 and 3 wing guard positions (Diagram 6-18). Note that the wing guards are moved out farther than the free-throw line extended.

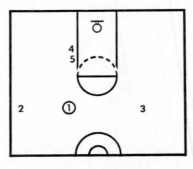

Diagram 6-18.

The primary function of 1 is to get the ball to the bottom man on the stack. 2 and 3 were told to move to the baseline or to the basket anytime their defensive men would try to help 4 and 5 or to rotate away from the Stack positions (Diagram 6-19).

4 would break around the screen being set by 5 for a pass from 1. Then, 1 would clear out away from the two men. 4 would try to get the shot, drive either left or right, or try to pass to 5 and cut. Basically, the two men would play two-man basketball until they got a good high-percentage shot.

Diagram 6-19.

The tempo used was ball control because of the lack of experience of the three remaining players.

The Goofy Stack team won handily in the scrimmage. Later, we modified the offense where the point man would call "Goofy Stack" from the basic 1-2-2 offensive formation and the post men would form the Post Stack and the play would be run.

One of the problems with the offense is that it is not a complete team offense and a coach probably would not want to use the offense through-out an entire game. However, it is worthy of use in order to add a change of pace or a new dimension to the basic offense.

THE OFFENSIVE INDEX

Our Offensive Index Outline is presented to give coaches an idea of how we established our master plan for the offensive options we used. This method has been very helpful in planning our weekly and daily practice plans.

OFFENSIVE INDEX CHART

I.   Man-to-Man Offense

    A.   Pass and Cut-Basic Offense. (Options started with Wing guards.) The wing guard has the following options:

        1. To shoot the set or jump shot;

        2. To drive the baseline;

        3. To drive the middle and force switch by post men;

        4. To pass to 1 cutting through;

        5. Pass to 4 and cut to the baseline (give and go);

        6. Pass to 4 and cut to the middle. If cutter does not get the ball back, go screen for the off-side wing guard;

        7. Call the name of the post man on your side who will come out and set a screen on your defensive man. Pick and roll;

        8. Call "Roll It" and the post man on your side goes away and screens for the post man on the opposite side of the lane;

        9. Call "Fan It" and the post men exchange positions without a screen;

10. Call "Away" and the post men exchange positions in reverse manner than "Fan It"; or

11. Call "Twist." Post man on opposite side moves up high to set up a screen by the post man on the ball side. After screening, the post man reverses back to low post on the ball side of the court.

B. Center Guard Outside

1. Left
2. Right

C. Automatics

1. Pass to 4 and screen for 3
2. Pass to 5 and screen for 2

D. Clearout Series

1. Regular Clear
2. Signal Clear
3. 4 Clear
4. 5 Clear

E. Red Offense

1. Basic Rotation and Cuts
2. Change Position Options

F. Special Plays

1. Double (Left and Right)
2. Blue
3. Post
4. Quick
5. Wide
6. Goofy Stack

II. Zone Offense

A. Against 1-2-2 Zone Defense

1. 1-4 Blitz-Rotate
2. Basic 1-2-2—Wildcat Rotation
3. 2-1-2 Spot-Up Series
4. Baseline Overload

B.   Against 2-1-2 Zone Defense

1. 1-4 Blitz Rotate
2. Basic 1-2-2—Wildcat Rotation
3. 1-3-1 Spot-Up
4. 1-3-1 Rotation

C.   Against 1-3-1 Zone Defense

1. 1-4 Blitz Rotate
2. Baseline Overload
3. 2-1-2 Spot-Up

D.   Against Match-Up Defense

1. 1-4 Blitz-Rotate
2. Basic 1-2-2 Plus Regular Man-to-Man Plays
3. Red Cat Shuffle

E.   Against Combination Defenses

1. 1-4 Blitz Rotate
2. Basic 1-2-2
3. Red Cat Shuffle

F.   Delay Situations

1. Four Corner
2. Run Regular Patterns—Take Only Lay-ups

III. Auxiliary Offense

A.   Out-of-Bounds Plays

1. 44 (Zone)
2. 43 (Man-to-Man)
3. Box Series
    a. Over
    b. Out
    c. Across
    d. Slide (Zone)

B.   Full-Court Press Offense

1. Pass and Go Away
2. Pass and Hold
3. Pass and Cut to Open Spot
4. Man-to-Man

C. Jump-Ball Alignments

   1. Offensive I
   2. Box
   3. Diamond
   4. Y

D. Delay or Control Tempo Offenses

   1. Red Offensive Series against a Man-to-Man
   2. Pass and Cut without Shooting against Man-to-Man
   3. Spot-Up Series (Zone)
   4. Stack Zone Series

E. One Shot Plays

   1. Clearout Series (Man-to-Man)
   2. Red Offensive Series (Man-to-Man)
   3. Overload (Zones)
   4. 1-4 Blitz and Rotate against zones
   5. Inside Out against zones

CHAPTER 7

Running the Wheel Series
from the 1-2-2

The Wheel Offense was developed in a book by Garland Pinholster, former head basketball coach at Oglethorpe College in Atlanta, Georgia. My interest in this shuffle-type offense developed as a result of seeing several outstanding battles between Oglethorpe and Carson-Newman College in Jefferson City, Tennessee. Dick Campbell, head basketball coach at Carson-Newman, ran a variation of the Wheel which he had modified from the Wheel. I was impressed with the constant screening and movement that occurred on the basic options. The material presented in this chapter was accumulated from notes I gathered over the years while following the two above-mentioned teams. We use the Wheel from the 1-2-2 formation and have added several additional cuts to meet our particular needs.

There are several features of the Wheel offense that should help sell the offensive series to coaches who have not used the Shuffle concepts before. These features include:

1. Tempo flexibility.
2. Excellent for team with a lack of height.
3. Constant movement of personnel.
4. High percentage shots only.
5. Helps develop good ball handling team.
6. Flexibility in substituting players.

Tempo Flexibility

By tempo flexibility, we mean the offense may be used as a highly disciplined tempo control attack or may be used with the fast break as a quick-hitting, high-scoring offense. The material a coach has on hand will determine the offensive tempo to be used.

We have used this series as a delay game or at other times, when we want to run some time off the clock when we have the lead but do not want to play for the foul by the opponents. We will give instructions to take only the lay-up shot in these situations.

If we are trying to speed up the tempo defensively, we will press, usually man-to-man with run-and-jump principles, and open up the offense by encouraging the quick shots, either on the lay-ups or the jump shots as soon as each player receives a pass.

Excellent for Team with Lack of Height

When we first began installing the Wheel Series, we started teaching the basic patterns to our freshman and junior varsity squads and used the offense as a ball-handling drill with our varsity squad. By the middle of the first year, our varsity was executing so well that we began using the Wheel exclusively.

The second season we were faced with a squad with only two players over six-feet tall. Our guards were 5'7" and 5'9" and 6'0", and our two post men were 6'2" and 6'3" (147 lbs.) The team was extremely quick so we combined the Wheel with a fast break and a pressing defense. The team compiled a 23—1 regular season record with a high state rating. This team reached the sub-state round before being eliminated from tournament play.

Constant Movement of Personnel

One of the reasons we went to the Wheel Series was to keep our players moving and changing positions because of our lack of height. We wanted to take our opponents' big men away from the basket so our smaller, quicker team could beat them to the goal for the rebound. Our team outrebounded every team on our schedule except three, and held one big, high-ranked team scoreless in one quarter while scoring 21 points themselves. The rebound ratio was 37 to 21 in our favor, despite going against a 6'6", 6'5" and 6'4" front line. Our 6'3" center, weighing 147 pounds, collected 21 rebounds against the 6'6", 225 pound post man by beating this man to the boards throughout the game.

All five men are moving as the ball swings from side to side. The Auburn Shuffle, made popular in the 1950's by Coach Joel Eaves at Auburn University, was the forerunner of the Wheel. Coach Eaves used all five men in his rotation offense. All five men would be playing in all five positions at one time or another during the offensive sequences with the big center handling the ball at the guard spot. The Wheel uses four men in the rotation and allows the big man to stay inside for rebounding purposes.

High-Percentage Shots Only

One of the coaching tips I have mentioned frequently throughout this book is to use only options that will give our team a high-percentage shot. As a coach, I do not believe it is necessary to take shots beyond the top of the free-throw circle. Our teams have averaged over 43 percent from the field over the past 15 years and frequently are in the high forties. Our top percentage was 49 percent. This includes the percentages of all substitutes who generally shoot lower percentages because of their inexperience.

Another reason we stress taking only good-percentage shots is the experience we have had with some of our opponents over the years. Many teams with big scoring stars will try to maintain their scoring averages even at the expense of the team's shooting percentage. Several years ago, we were playing a team in our conference who had the city's leading scorer with a 27 point average. The player became so concerned with his average that he began forcing shots which we recovered. The player got his average, but we won the game by 17 points and the star scorer hit only 30 percent of his field goal attempts. This same illustration has happened many times throughout the years.

With the Wheel Series, there is no reason for low shooting percentages. If a starter or regular player drops below 40 percent we study our game video tapes to see if the player is taking low-percentage shots. We point this out to the player and also assign additional shooting before our formal section of practice begins.

In the final analysis, if an offensive pattern does not provide good percentage shots, the pattern should be eliminated from the offense.

Helps Develop Good Ball-Handling Team

One of the side benefits we discovered when installing the Wheel Series was the improvement of our team's ball handling ability. Because of the constant movement of players and the passing involved, good team ball handling will come naturally. Players meeting all passes are taught to time their cuts and set up the defensive man, thus becoming good pass receivers. The passers are taught to read the defensive man and make the pass on the shoulder away from the defensive man.

The Wheel basic cut was first used in our program as a ball-handling drill and defensive drill to teach our off-side defensive man how to apply pressure on cutters and how to deny passes in the post area. We also wanted to play defense against the offense because we saw the offense several times during the year. Most teams in our area that used the Wheel ran it from a 2-1-2 alignment like the Carson-Newman offense used by Dick Campbell. From our experiences in practice, we feel the offense has made several valuable contributions to both our offensive and defensive development.

Flexibility in Substituting Players

Another key feature of the Wheel Series is the substituting of players. Four positions are interchangeable. This allows the coach to use his bench more easily than in many standard offenses. This feature may be quite beneficial if the squad lacks height.

We have mentioned many of the plus features of the offense. There have been three areas of weakness that should be noted. Counter arguments have already been presented against these disadvantages which a coach must weigh in making a decision on using the Wheel Series.

1. Offensive rebounding weaker.
2. Defensive and safety assignments more difficult to master.
3. All players must be good ball handlers.

Offensive Rebounding Weaker

The constant continuity of the Wheel takes the rebounders outside more than our Basic 1-2-2 pattern. However, we feel that a smaller, quicker team can overcome this weakness because of the reasons previously discussed in this chapter.

Defensive and Safety Assignments More Difficult to Master

Since we have placed heavy emphasis .on our rebounding the offensive board and protecting against our opponents' fast break, the Wheel Series presents somewhat of a problem in filling these assignments. The man who rotates out front is assigned the safety position, and the wing man making a baseline pass rotates to the outlet pass spot. One disadvantage results because a big forward and excellent rebounder may rotate out front. We would prefer him to rebound. Also, we would prefer our quicker, smaller point man to be out front. We think we have the fast break better covered and our chances of obtaining the offensive rebound are slightly weakened by the Wheel Series. However, the Wheel presents excellent opportunities which may overcome the disadvantages presented, and a coach must take all of the factors into consideration when choosing an offensive series that will afford his team the best chance to win.

All Players Must Be Good Ball Handlers

Since at least four men are involved in the continuity of the Wheel, each player must be a good ball handler. This could create problems for the coach. However, we feel the coach should have several good ball handlers before he selects this series to add to his offensive system. This follows our philosophy of adopting the offense to meet the needs of the existing personnel.

Another factor which helps overcome this disadvantage is the pattern, and the practice time it takes to install the pattern will make better ball handlers out of each player. The basic Wheel may be used as a drill to help develop the necessary ball handling to successful use of the Wheel offensive series.

The basic player alignment of the Wheel Series is the standard 1-2-2 alignment that has been used throughout the preceding chapters.

Diagram 7-1 shows the entry pass being made from 1 to 3 at the right wing guard position. 4, upon seeing the entry pass being completed, quickly moves across the free-throw lane area to set a stationary screen on 2's defensive man. 2 fakes to the baseline (steps with the left foot), pushes off on his left foot, and cuts over the top of the screen by 4 to the basket. This is the first option on the 1-2-2 Wheel cut.

1, after passing to 3, moves down to screen for 4 and 5 (Diagram 7-2). Immediately after screening for 2, 4 cuts around a moving screen

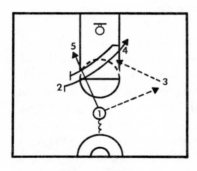

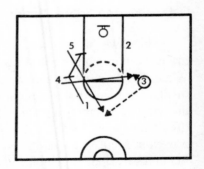

Diagram 7-1.   Diagram 7-2.

being set by 1 and goes to the high side post area on the ball side. 1 continues on down the left side of the free-throw lane and screens for 5, who cuts to the top of the circle. There will be times when 5 will have a high-percentage shot from the free-throw line as soon as he receives the ball from 3.

One special tip should be included at this point. It has been my experience with the Shuffle or Wheel type offensive series that the players become so pattern conscious they will not take advantage of the good shot or driving opportunity. Coaches using this offensive series for the first time should constantly encourage their players to recognize the shot possibilities and hit the good shot whenever it comes open. A good drill is to have five offensive players run through the basic cuts and have the coach call the time when each player will possibly have a good shot. For example, have 2 shoot on the first cut, 5 on the cut to the top of the circle, 4 drop-step and drive back in the lane, etc.

To change the continuity back to the opposite side of the court, 3 passes to 5, who quickly dribbles to his left to set up a pass to 1. A coaching point we stress with the man outside (5 in this example) is for the man receiving the ball to cross the ball quickly in front of his body and dribble with the left hand. This maneuver will allow 5 (the outside man) to move from one side of the lane to the other with only one dribble necessary. As soon as 3 passes the ball to 5, 2 moves out about two steps from the right edge of the free-throw lane to set a stationary screen for 3. 1 cuts out toward the left wing guard position to receive a pass from 5. As the pass is made, 3 cuts off the screen being set by 2. Usually, the cut will be made along the baseline side of the screen. 1 may shoot after receiving the pass

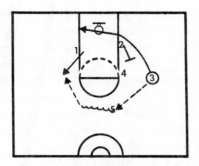

Diagram 7-3.

from 5, dribble to the basket (3 holds cut if he sees the drive to the basket), or pass to 3 (Diagram 7-3).

One of the defensive strategies we face is tight defensive pressure on the pass from 5 to 1. To counter this pressure, 1 will cut hard to the ball and then reverse to the basket if being heavily overplayed. 5 must be able to read the defense and be ready to make the pass on the reverse cut. After reversing and cutting to the basket, 1 may again cut out to receive the pass at the wing position. 3 must delay his baseline cut until the reverse has been completed or the pass is made to 1 at the wing position. This two-man reverse should be incorporated into the breakdown drill section of the daily practice. All players should be taught to make the reverse cut and the pass to the cutter because all players will find themselves in one of the two positions in the offensive continuity.

If the reverse cut was not used, 5 passes to 1 at the left wing guard position (Diagram 7-4). 2 screens for 3 who cuts to the basket as shown in

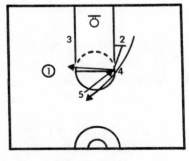

Diagram 7-4.

Diagram 7-3. 5 immediately screens to the opposite direction from his pass to 1 for 4 and then for 2. 4 cuts to the side high-post position where he may receive a pass from 1 and run the post split option shown in Diagram 7-6. 2 cuts to the top of the free-throw circle. 1 may hit the first cutter, 3; pass to 4 and split; or pass outside to 2. Any of the players who receive a pass from 1 should look for the scoring opportunities.

Diagram 7-5 shows additional continuity as 1 passes the ball to 2 at the top of the free-throw circle. 5 breaks out to the right wing guard position to receive a pass from 2. As soon as the pass is completed, 4 sets a stationary screen on 1's defensive man and 1 cuts over the top of the screen to the basket looking for a pass from 5. 2, after passing to 5, hesitates until 1 has completed his cut over the screen by 4, and then screens for 4, who cuts to the high side position. 2 continues on down the lane to screen for 3, who cuts to the top of the circle. If 5 does not pass to the first cutter (1) or to the post cutter (4), he may pass to 3 at the top of the circle to swing the ball back to the left side of the court as the continuity proceeds.

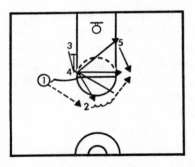

Diagram 7-5.

So far in this chapter, all of the diagrams have shown the basic continuity. Diagram 7-6 shows one of the options that may be run anytime the ball is passed to the side high post man. On the post option in Diagram 7-6, 3 passes to 4 and fakes a cut to the baseline and cuts back to split the post man 4. He may receive a return pass or screen for 5 who cuts off the screen for a possible pass from 4. If 5 gets the ball for the drive or jump shot, 2 must clear out by moving across the lane. If 5 pulls up and shoots the jump shot or cannot shoot, 2 screens for 1 on the baseline. 5 may pass

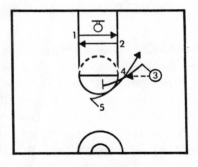

Diagram 7-6.

the ball back to 4 on the pick-and-roll as 4 slides down the lane after passing to 5.

If 4 does not pass the ball to the two split men 3 or 5, he may pass the ball back out front to 3 to continue the basic pattern. In Diagram 7-7, 4 passes to 3 who takes the dribble to the left and passes to 2 who breaks out to the left wing guard position. 1 sets a screen for 5 who cuts along the baseline to receive a pass from 2. 3 will then screen for 4 and move down to screen again for 1. As the Wheel option continues, 2 may shoot, drive, pass to 5, the baseline cutter, pass to 4 or out front to 1 (Diagram 7-8).

Diagram 7-7.

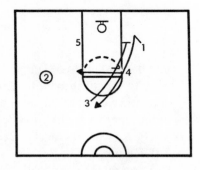

Diagram 7-8.

One key feature of the Wheel Series is the ease with which the continuity may be restarted after a counter-option has been used.

SPECIAL OPTIONS USED WITH BASIC WHEEL SERIES

All offensive series must have a certain amount of variety. The following are options that have been used successfully with the basic series to add a new dimension to offense.

In order to counter the over-play technique used by the opponent's defense, we installed the Strong-side Option shown in Diagrams 7-9 and 7-10. With the ball at the left wing guard spot, 2 passes back out front to 1. 1 dribbles once toward the right side of the court to make it appear the regular rotation is being run, then reverses back to the left side. 2, seeing the reverse, sets a screen on 5 who cuts out to the left wing position for a pass from 1. 5 often gets the short jump shot off this pass if 5 sets up his cut properly by faking into the lane prior to cutting behind the screen by 2 (Diagram 7-9).

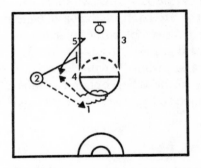

Diagram 7-9.

After passing to 5, 1 cuts to the basket around a screen being set by 4. 5 passes to 1, cutting to the basket. This quick option has provided several lay-ups and should be incorporated into the basic series. 2 must clear out by moving across the free-throw lane. 3 rotates out to the position vacated by 1. The basic rotation may be continued merely by passing the ball back to 3 (Diagram 7-10).

A special Pick and Roll Option may be keyed by the wing man with the ball calling the name of the side high post man. In Diagram 7-10, 5 calls the name of the 4 man who steps out to set a screen on 5's defensive man. 5 drives to the free-throw lane area looking for a drive to the basket or

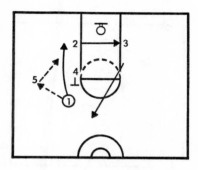

Diagram 7-10.

a jump shot. 4 rolls out to the basket after 5 has dribbled past the screen. 4 may receive a pass from 5 on the roll to the basket. 1 must cut out of his position to the corner to clear his man out of the area. 3 screens away for 2 who fills the outside position (Diagram 7-11).

This option is suggested when a team has a good jump shooter from the outside. Also, a team's best offensive man may be better used with the Pick and Roll option. All of the special options shown may be run on either side of the court.

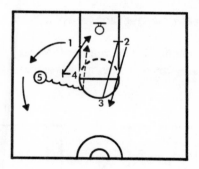

Diagram 7-11.

To reset if a good shot has not been taken, 5 passes to 2 out front and then fills the baseline screening position. 4 returns to the high post position (Diagram 7-12). The Wheel Series rotation is now ready to be run again.

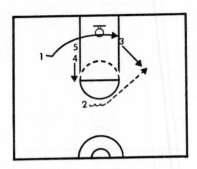

Diagram 7-12.

One of the problems the offense encounters is tight pressure on the entry passes to either wing guard. This becomes more of a problem if the opponent's defensive wing guards are quicker than the offensive wing guards. The Release pattern was added to counter this pressure. 1, if seeing the wing guards are being overplayed, calls "Release." 2 and 3 move quickly to screen inside for 4 and 5 who both cut outside to the wing spots (Diagram 7-13). 1 passes to 4. 3 moves quickly across the free-throw lane to set a screen for 5 who cuts through the lane for a possible pass from 4. 1 now screens for 3 who cuts to the ball to become the side high post man. 1 continues down the lane to screen for 2 who cuts to the high post area (Diagram 7-14).

This is an excellent time to run the "Name" option described in Diagram 7-10 because of the movement created by the Release play.

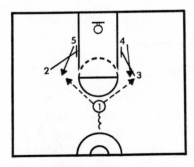

Diagram 7-13.

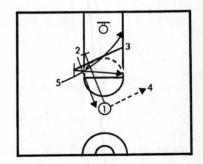

Diagram 7-14.

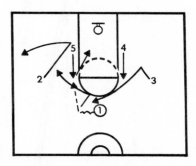

Diagram 7-15.

Another maneuver to counter the defensive pressure on the wing guards was inserted. This maneuver is called the "Backdoor Release" and is keyed when "Post" is called by the point man 1. On hearing the call by 1, both post men, 5 and 4, move up quickly to the high post areas on each side of the free-throw lane. 1 hits 5(Diagram 7-15). 2 cuts backdoor to the basket as soon as he sees the pass from 1 to 5. 5 pivots to the outside and passes to 2 cutting to the basket. 5 may also use the drop step and drive to the basket. We have used this maneuver very successfully when 5 is a good driving post man and we encounter tough man-to-man pressure. If 2 does not receive a pass from 5, 1 cuts outside 5 and may receive a pass from 5. A pick-and-roll to the basket option may be employed between 1 and 5. After returning the ball to 1, 5 rolls to the basket. If 1 shoots, we have 5 on the offensive boards.

A third option is run when 1, after cutting by 5 without getting the ball, screens for 2 who cuts back behind 1's screen for a short jump shot (Diagram 7-16). 2 may also pass to 1 as we post the point man. This is a good offensive technique if the opponents use a small guard on our point man 1.

A fourth special play that has been used successfully is the "Quick" play (Diagram 7-17). The play is keyed by 1 who dribbles to the left and calls "Quick." 4 cuts hard to the free-throw line to receive a pass from 1. 4 pivots toward the side he cut from and looks for 3, reverse-cutting quickly to the basket. We have been able to hit 3 for a cheap basket. After passing to 4, 1 cuts around 4 and may receive a return pass from him. If not, 1 becomes the low man who will break out to the wing guard position if 4 decides to continue the Wheel pattern.

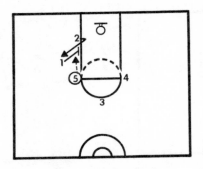

Diagram 7-16.

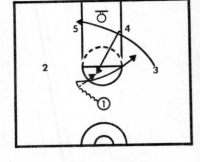

Diagram 7-17.

To reset the offense, 4 passes to 1, 3 screens for 2 who cuts along the baseline to the basket. 5 moves up the free-throw lane to fill the post position (Diagram 7-18).

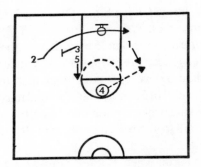

Diagram 7-18.

The fifth special play is called the "Flood" play (Diagram 7-19). The point man 1 calls "Flood," passes to the wing guard 3 and goes outside for a return pass from 3. While this exchange is happening, 5 moves across the free-throw lane and sets a double screen for 3 who, after handing the ball back to 1, cuts around the double screen for the return lob pass from 1. 2 rotates out to the top of the circle as defensive safety and as a possible pass receiver. The Flood play requires exact timing and should be practiced frequently in order to be effective. It is a good play when the team has an excellent leaper in the 3 spot. The Flood play may be run on either side of the court with equal results.

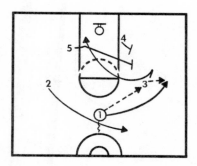

Diagram 7-19.

If 1 did not throw the lob pass to 3 on the Flood Special, he passes out front to 2 and cuts over the top of the same double screen used by 3. 2 can pass to 1 or to 3 who had cut to the left wing guard position. 3 may pass to 1 as the Wheel pattern continues (Diagram 7-20).

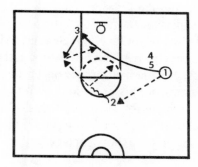

Diagram 7-20.

Diagram 7-21 shows the remaining off-side action and the moves to set up the wheel rotation. 2, after passing to 3, screens for 5 who cuts to the side high post position and for 4 who cuts to the head of the circle to become the point man on the change of sides.

Coaches planning to incorporate the Special Play Options to the Wheel Series should be careful not to put in too many plays. Be sure the team can execute each play successfully before adding another new option. All players must be familiar with every option used in order to develop the desired timing and good offensive results.

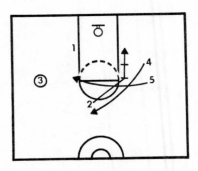

Diagram 7-21.

There are two additional Wheel variations we used before we began using the five Special Plays previously described. These two variations are called the "Post" and "Forward" variations.

The main purpose of these two options is to counter the opponent's tendency to switch on the off-side exchange between the man at the top of the free-throw circle and the off-side man.

Diagram 7-22 shows the first option on the Post variation. 1 passes to 3. 4 moves across the free-throw lane and sets a screen for 2 who cuts to the basket for a possible pass from 3. This is the same as the first option on the regular Wheel Series. The main difference occurs as 5 cuts directly to the high side post position from his off-side position. 1, after passing and delaying two counts, screens for 4 who cuts to the point position. 1 moves on down to become the off-side man. Wing guard 3 may pass to 2, 5, or out front to 4. 4 will be able to get a shot or at least get an easier pass from 3.

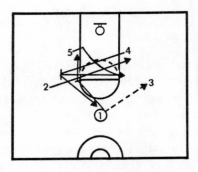

Diagram 7-22.

To continue the Post variation, 3 passes to 4 who dribbles back to the left and passes to 1 who cuts out to the wing spot as 4 begins his dribble. 2 screens for 3 who cuts to the basket on the baseline side. After screening, 2 cuts quickly to the high side post position for a possible pass from 1. 4 screens for 5 who rotates out front. 4 moves on down to become the off-side man (Diagram 7-23).

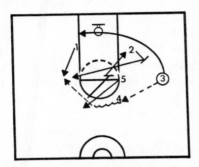

Diagram 7-23.

This variation can catch the defense by surprise and can break a tight game open with a few quick baskets. We use these variations for about two to three minutes and go back to the original Wheel Series. The variations, when they yield a couple of quick baskets, make the defense play the original options more honestly, thus helping eliminate the tendency to play the pattern rather than play the man.

The Forward variation is shown in Diagrams 7-24 and 7-25. 1 passes

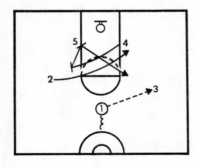

Diagram 7-24.

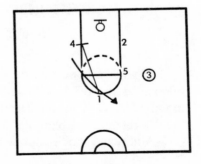

Diagram 7-25.

to 3. 4 moves across the lane to set a screen on 2, who cuts to the basket. 4 then reverses and sets a second screen on 5 who cuts to the side high post area. 3 may hit 2 on the first option or 5 cutting into the post area. A quick jump shot may be available at this point for 5 (Diagram 7-23). 1 screens away for 4 who moves to the high post position (Diagram 7-24). This variation gives the original offense a slightly different appearance and may produce a few quick baskets which can turn the game around.

Coaching Suggestions

The coach planning to use the Wheel Series should first study the offense thoroughly. He must learn all of the minute details that help make the plays successful.

The next suggestion is to know your personnel. Many coaches see college teams run beautiful offensive patterns and copy them without taking into consideration that colleges try to recruit players to meet the specific needs of the system of offense the coach is running. Coaches below the college level must adapt their offenses to the available personnel and often the talent is not available to run a complicated offensive system.

The third suggestion for the coach is to avoid putting in too many plays. Make sure your players fully understand what you are trying to do and are able to execute the offense efficiently. Use only the options that your team can execute correctly.

The Wheel Series is a great offensive system if used wisely. It demands a total commitment and can produce instant results if coupled with a good, sound defensive system.

MODIFIED REBOUNDING AND DEFENSIVE
SAFETY ASSIGNMENTS

When we converted our offensive system from our Basic 1-2-2 offense to the offensive 1-2-2 Wheel Series, we also installed the modified Rebounding and Defensive Safety Assignment Plans. We used the 3-2 rebounding plan discussed in Chapter 1.

Additional modifications included the following rules:

1. The side high post man always rebounds the front position.

2. The wing guard passing the ball to the cutter and the man who rotates to the head of the circle become the two outlet pass and safety men.

3. The cutter taking the shot rebounds in the low ball-side position.

4. The man screening for the off-side man (original screener) will rebound the low off-side positions.

These four basic rules will handle all of the offensive and defensive safety assignments on each of the Wheel options. All players should be thoroughly drilled in these rules and must execute them correctly. This simplified rebounding plan will provide even more high-percentage shots and make the Wheel Series provide the necessary tools for winning more basketball games.

CHAPTER 8

Attacking the Man-to-Man Defense with the 1-2-2 Scramble Series

The Scramble Series was created primarily to vary the entry points of the basic 1-2-2 offense in order to counter pressure man-to-man defensive techniques. This became a problem when we had tall, but slow, wing guards who were being covered by much quicker defensive men. The main objective of the series is to move all four players, except the point man, to new positions on the court, then make the entry pass to the players in the new positions. This technique proved highly effective in achieving our initial objective.

As we added other options we discovered more benefits to the series. More movement cut down on the sluffing or off-side defensive help because the defensive players had to keep up with our players now on the move.

The Scramble Series also provided several new ways to conceal our basic offense. This feature allowed us to hide certain plays that were working well by running the same plays from different positions. Our offense appeared to be more complicated as a result and made the opponents' defensive assignments more difficult.

The Scramble Series may be used as the first cuts for all of the different offensive series in this book.

THE REGULAR SCRAMBLE CONCEALMENT

The Scramble options may be used by pre-arrangement with the coach, or by the point man, seeing heavy defensive pressure on the two offensive wing guards, calling the Scramble Series. The initial call by the point man 1 is "Scramble." Upon hearing the call, wing guards 2 and 3 cut directly to the low post positions and post men 4 and 5 cut to the high post positions just outside the free-throw lane in the high side post spots (Diagram 8-1). The entry pass may now be made to either 4 or 5.

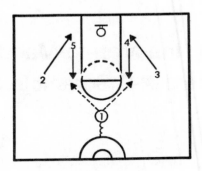

Diagram 8-1.

If the entry pass is made to 4, 1 cuts outside (Diagram 8-2). 4 pivots to the inside as 5 screens down the lane for 2. 2 sets up the screen by step-faking into the lane before cutting around the screen by 5. 4 passes to 2 if he is open. After screening for 2, 5 reverses back into the lane for a possible pass from 4.

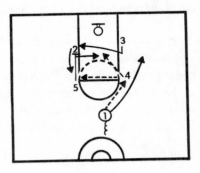

Diagram 8-2.

If 4 passes to 2, 5 sets a screen for 3. 3 must set up the cut along the baseline by faking in the direction of 4. 2 passes to 3 on the baseline for the

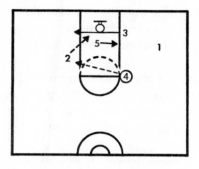

Diagram 8-3.

possible shot (Diagram 8-3). The screen by 5 is a moving screen because it is being set in the three-second area of the free-throw lane. The timing is important because of this factor and the possibility of setting an illegal screen. The coach should stress both of these points in teaching this phase of the option.

Diagram 8-4 shows the entry pass being made to 5. 1 cuts to the outside after the pass. 5 pivots to the inside. 4 screens down the lane for 3 who fakes inside the lane before cutting around 4's screen. 5 passes the ball to 3 if he is open. 4 reverses back into the lane for a possible pass from 5. If 3 receives a pass from 5 but does not have the shot, 4 sets a moving screen for 2 in the lane area avoiding the previously mentioned pitfalls (Diagram 8-5).

2 should set up his cut with a moving step fake up toward the free-throw lane. Coaches should constantly stress the step fake away from

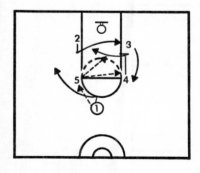

Diagram 8-4.

Diagram 8-5.

the direction of the intended cut. This fake should be made in a direction that might confuse or delay the defensive man.

We have found the baseline cut to be highly effective in producing the good shot.

If 1 did not pass to either post man on the Scramble call, 1 calls "Down." 4 and 5 pivot and screen down the lane for the wing guards 2 and 3. 2 and 3 set up their cuts around the screens. 1 may pass to either man for the quick jump shot or drive (Diagram 8-6).

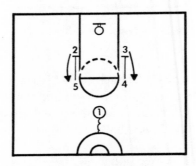

Diagram 8-6.

Note: The two options may produce the high-percentage shots if executed properly. Stress the details of faking before cutting for more effective use of the Scramble.

If 1 passes to 3, he cuts outside. 3 pivots back to the inside as 2 screens down the lane for 5, who cuts around the screen for a possible pass from 3.

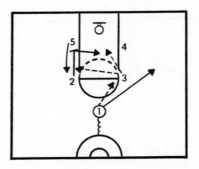

Diagram 8-7.

2 reverses into the lane area and may also receive a pass from 3 (Diagram 8-7).

Diagram 8-8 shows a further breakdown after 3 passes to 5. 2 continues across the free-throw lane and screens for 4 who fakes and cuts behind the screen set by 2. 5 passes to 4 on the baseline.

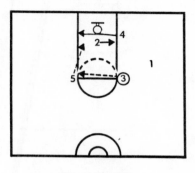

Diagram 8-8.

If 1 passes to 2, he cuts outside. 3 screens down the lane for 4 who fakes and cuts around the screen to receive a possible pass from 2. 3 reverses into the lane and may also receive a pass from 2 (Diagram 8-9). Diagram 8-10 shows a continuation of the option described in Diagram 8-9. 3 sets a screen for 5 who cuts along the baseline for a pass from 4.

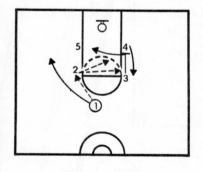

Diagram 8-9.

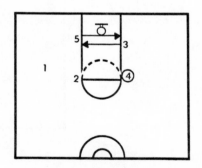

Diagram 8-10.

The next Scramble option is called "Scramble Across." The purpose again is to give additional movement to the four players without the ball. 1 calls "Scramble Across." 4 and 5 move up to the high side post positions where they may receive a pass from 1. Wing guards 2 and 3 cut to the low post positions on the opposite side of the court from their original wing positions (Diagram 8-11).

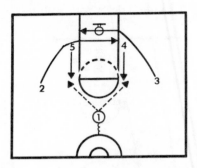

Diagram 8-11.

If the entry pass is made to post man 4 by 1, the following options occur (Diagram 8-12): 5 screens down the lane for 3, who fakes into the lane and cuts around behind the screen for a possible pass from 4. After screening, 5 reverses into the lane and also may receive a pass from 4. 1 cuts outside 4 after the initial entry pass.

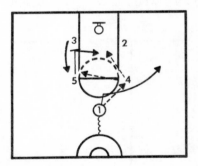

Diagram 8-12.

The final option in the pattern is the baseline cut by 2. If the ball is passed to 3 and the shot is not taken, 5 continues on across the free-throw lane and sets a moving screen on 2's defensive man. 2 fakes and cuts along

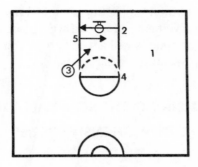

Diagram 8-13.

the baseline for a possible pass from 3. This is basically the same play as shown in Diagram 8-2, except the wing guards have interchanged positions.

If the entry pass goes to 5 after the "Scramble Across" call by the point man, 1 goes outside to clear the area. 4 screens down the lane for 2, who fakes and cuts around the screen for a possible pass from 5. 4, after screening, reverses into the lane area for a quick pass from 5 (Diagram 8- 14).

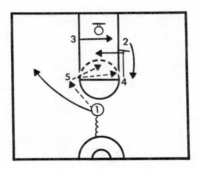

Diagram 8-14.

The final option in this sequence is for 4 to continue across the free-throw lane and screen for 3. 5 passes to 2 who quickly passes to 3 on the baseline for a possible shot (Diagram 8- 14).

The point man 1 may call "Scramble Across" and then call "Down" and the post men will repeat the option shown in Diagram 8- 6.

The Scramble options alone constitute a variety of good offensive plays with a lot of player movement and several high-percentage opportunities. Effective use of these options will depend on how well a coach drills his team on the ability to score off the set plays.

COMBINING THE SCRAMBLE WITH
OTHER OFFENSIVE SERIES

To achieve the maximum results from the Scramble Series, it should be combined with other offensive series shown in this book. This section will show how this may be accomplished and how well the Scramble Series complements the other options in the 1-2-2 offense.

Combining the Scramble and the Regular Clearout Option

In Diagram 8-15, we have shown the initial positions after 1 called "Scramble." The squad had been told we were combining the two plays so they knew we would run the appropriate clearout option after the initial scramble cut if the entry pass was successful. 1 passes to 4 and cuts outside

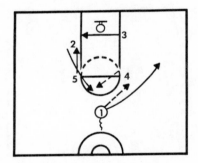

Diagram 8-15.

him for a possible return pass. 5 screens down the lane for 2, who comes to the free-throw line for a return pass from 4. Meanwhile, 3 has moved across the free-throw line to form the Swing Option Stack from the original option.

The new positions are shown in Diagram 8-16. As soon as 2 gets the

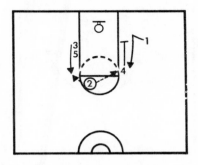

Diagram 8-16.

ball, 3 will swing-cut around 5 and if open will get a pass from 2 for the shot. 4, after passing to 2, moves down the right side of the free-throw lane and screens for 1 who has moved into a position near the basket. This screen by 4 sets up the Double Swing option described in Chapter 2. 2 may also add the dribble weave by taking the ball to 1 on the dribble.

As you can see, the Scramble can add a whole new dimension to the Clearout Series. When you go back to the original series, it will be much easier to run because of the confusion created by the Scramble option.

The same clearout plays may be executed with the entry pass being made to 5 or to either 2 or 3 after the Scramble Across and Down calls have been made. The Scramble Series provides eight different entries into any series a coach may choose to run.

Combining the Scramble with the Red Cat Shuffle

One of the most successful offensive series shown in this book is presented in Chapter 5. This series, called the Red Cat Shuffle, is a fast-moving, shuffle-type continuity offense with excellent scoring opportunities. Using the Scramble options as additional entry points into the offense has proved quite successful.

Diagram 8-17 illustrates the first option off the Red Cat Shuffle after 1 has called "Scramble" and the other four players have assumed their new positions. 1 passes to 4 and cuts outside him to clear out the front area. 5, after seeing the pass go to 4, steps out toward the left wing guard position. The purpose of this move is to set up the screen being set on his defensive man by 2. 3 must also take two steps away from the free-throw

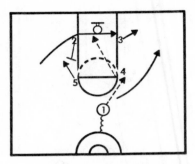

Diagram 8-17.

lane. 5 cuts behind the screen by 2 to the basket and looks for a possible pass from 4.

The second phase is shown in Diagram 8-18. 2, after screening for 5, cuts to the free-throw line, receives a pass from 4, and looks for the baseline cutter 3 who cuts behind a screen set just outside the lane area by 5. Again, all players should be encouraged to take the good shots whenever they occur on this series.

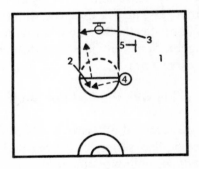

Diagram 8-18.

Diagram 8-19 shows the third phase of the Red Cat Shuffle. 4, after passing to 2, screens down the lane for 5 who cuts to the spot just vacated by 4. He should look for the shot possibilities as soon as he gets the ball. 2 screens for 3 to present 5 with the same pass as 2 had made previously to him.

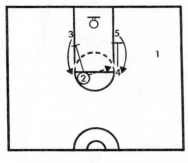

Diagram 8-19.

Combining the Scramble with the Wheel Options

The Scramble complements the Wheel Series by adding eight more ways to get into the basic patterns. This increase in entry options makes the wheel even more difficult to defense.

The first call is made by 1 who calls "Scramble." Diagram 8-20 shows the initial Scramble option. 2 and 3 cut to the low post spots while 4 and 5 move up to the high post positions possibly to receive a pass from 1. The next step is the entry pass to 5 by 1 (Diagram 8-21).

This option is similar to the Post Entry option to the Wheel Series shown in Chapter 7. 3 sets a rear stationary screen for 4 who cuts to the basket for a possible return pass from 5. After passing to 5, 1 screens opposite the basketball for 3, who cuts to the top of the free-throw circle to

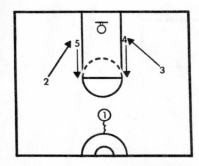

Diagram 8-20.

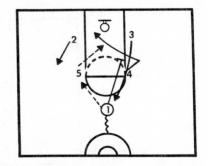

Diagram 8-21.

be the point man. 2 steps out to the left wing guard spot to set up the third step in the wheel continuity.

The quickness with which the Scramble entry and the conversion to the first wheel cut from the off side are the keys to getting the good shot. All cuts should be preceded by step fakes to set up the impending screens.

Diagram 8-22 illustrates the baseline cut. 5 passes to 3, who passes to 1, who has cut to the right wing guard position. 4 screens for 2 and 2 cuts along the baseline to the basket for a possible pass from 1.

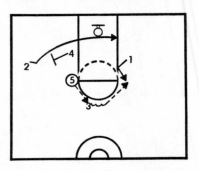

Diagram 8-22.

The off-side screens from Diagram 8-22 are shown in Diagram 8-23. After passing to 1, 3 screens for 5, who cuts to the side high post position. 3 continues on down the lane and sets a second screen on 4 who cuts to the top of the circle to the point position. 1 may pass to 2, to 5 and run the Post Split option, or pass back out front to 4 to continue the Wheel pattern to the left side of the court.

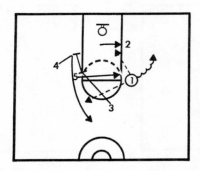

Diagram 8-23.

The same play may be run to the opposite side by making the entry pass to 4 instead of to 5. These diagrams will not be repeated since they are shown in Chapter 7 on the Wheel Series.

The next possibility is to combine the Scramble Down option and the Wheel. This entry option is started by 1 who calls "Scramble." After this option is completed, the point man 1 calls "Down." The post men move down the lane and both screen for wing guards 2 and 3 (Diagram 8-24). The wing guards cut around these screens and return to the high side post positions formerly filled by 4 and 5. This option resembles the Double Swing maneuvers shown in Chapter 3.

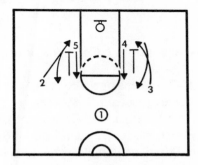

Diagram 8-24.

Diagram 8-25 shows the first option of the Wheel Series after the Scramble Down option has been completed. 1 passes to 2. 4 sets a rear stationary screen on 3's defensive man. 3 cuts to the basket over the top of the screen by 4. 5 moves out to the left wing spot to open up the lane area

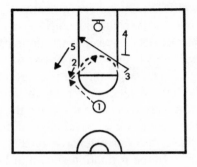

Diagram 8-25.

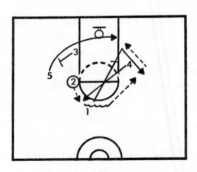

Diagram 8-26.

for 3, who may receive a pass from 2. Continuation of the option is shown in Diagram 8-26.

1, after passing to 2, screens opposite for 4. 4 cuts to the top of the free-throw circle to receive a pass from 2. 4 passes to 1. 3 screens for 5 who cuts to the basket on the baseline side (Diagram 8-26).

The same Wheel options may be run using the Scramble Across options. These Scramble options provide an additional four entry plays. The diagrams will not be duplicated since the basic options have already been shown in this chapter. Coaches can easily adapt these four additional Scramble Across options into the offensive system.

Combining the Scramble with the Weave

Several years ago, the dribble weave was a very popular offensive maneuver. As defenses began switching better, most coaches eliminated the dribble weave from their offensive systems.

We had one dribble weave pattern we named the "Loop" which helped provide our first district championship and my first 20-game-win season as a coach. Because of the reasons mentioned above, we dropped this pattern. Several seasons later, we were experimenting with three or four offensive series that we thought might fit our returning personnel and we used the Loop Dribble Weave pattern again.

Since no one in our area was currently using the dribble weave, we found this presented us with an excellent change of pace offense and we keep inserting the weave into our offensive system.

Players are aligned in the formation shown in Diagram 8-27 after

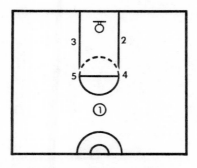

Diagram 8-27.

running the Scramble Across option shown in Diagram 8-11. The dribble weave can be initiated in two ways: (1) by a pass to 4 or 5 by 1, or (2) by an inside dribble by 1 handing off to either 4 or 5.

In Diagram 8-28, 1 begins the weave by passing to 5 and cutting to set a screen on 5's defensive man. 5 dribbles across the lane and hands off to 4 who sets up his defensive man with a step fake toward the basket. 4 should immediately look for a shot as he receives the pass from 5.

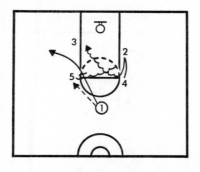

Diagram 8-28.

Diagram 8-29 shows a continuation of the weave pattern as 4 continues his dribble across the free-throw lane to pass to 3. 3 must read the defense and if he sees 4 has beaten his man, can drive on to the basket. If 3's defensive man switches to help with 4, 3 may receive a bounce pass for the power lay-up or the short jump shot.

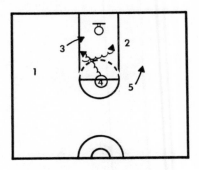

Diagram 8-29.

All of the entry passes of the Scramble Series may be used to start the Dribble Weave patterns. The dribble has the option to reverse and change directions at any time. This will create a difficult defensive adjustment for the opponents.

Another method to clear out 1 is shown in Diagram 8-30. 1 passes to 5 and cuts to the basket (Give and Go Play). 1 may cut either way if he does

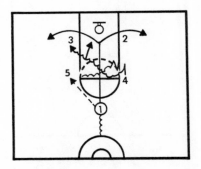

Diagram 8-30.

not get a return pass from 5. 5 begins the Dribble Weave option by dribbling inside of 4. 4 sets up the exchange by faking toward the basket before cutting around 5 for the dribble exchange. 4 drives to the basket and shoots if open or he may pass to either 2 or 3 if the defense switches.

A key coaching point must be stressed when using the weave. With each exchange, the ball should be taken as close to the basket as possible. Many teams running the weave have a tendency to dribble laterally from sideline to sideline which takes away the main objective of an offensive play—to get the basketball to the basket for a good shot as quickly as possible.

CHAPTER 9

The Blitz and Rotation Series
Against Zone Defenses

Attacking the various zone defenses encountered in today's complex game of basketball is one of the main problems the coach must solve. There are many types of standard zones, combination zone and man-to-man defenses and match-up defenses designed to confuse the offense. It is almost impossible for the coach to install an offensive series for each type of defense his team may face during the season. For this reason, coaches are constantly seeking an offense that can be easily adapted to meet these defensive challenges.

The 1-4 Blitz and Rotate Series to be presented in this chapter is the best single offensive series to be used against all types of zone defenses that we encounter. Several of the reasons for adopting the 1-4 Blitz and Rotate Series to our offensive system are:

1. Provides excellent entry pass possibilities;
2. Creates a strong inside attack;
3. Establishes good overload situations;
4. Allows for good outside shooting;
5. Combines excellent inside-outside attack possibilities in one pattern;
6. Adequate continuity;
7. Creates good, quick, high-percentage shots for every player; and
8. Extremely difficult for teams to match-up against without going to straight man-to-man.

Provides Excellent Entry Passes

One of the strong features of the 1-4 Blitz and Rotate attack is its versatility in initiating the pattern. There are four opportunities for the point men to begin the offense. No other formation provides such opportunities.

Creates Strong Inside Attack

As stated frequently throughout this book, I believe in taking the ball inside against every kind of defense and against every team we play. If our opponents have a big man, we believe in forcing him to play defense. Many coaches, in playing against teams with a big defensive center, will avoid going at the big man. These teams seem to be content with the good outside shot. However, I do not believe a team can win on outside shooting alone. The percentages are simply not in favor of the teams who shoot mostly from the outside areas.

For example, our 1974-75 Oak Ridge team's field goal percentage was 47 percent. The best outside shooter on the team shot 45 percent. Our two post men shot 52 percent and 55 percent respectively, and in addition, they received 86 and 97 free throws each. The three starting guards shot only 37, 51 and 55 free throws, each between them. Thus, the two post men, shooting a higher percentage from the field, drew more fouls than the three guards.

By the way, the two post men were 6'1" and 6'3" in height, respectively, and were out-rebounded only three games all season. The team out-rebounded the number-one ranked team in the state polls and pulled a major upset by scoring a 55-52 victory on a neutral floor.

Establishes Good Overload Situations

The principle of overloading a zone in one area has always been one of the most popular methods of attacking the various zone defenses. The idea is to get more offensive men in one area than the defense has, and move the ball to the open man. This method is used quite frequently at most levels of competition.

The 1-4 Blitz and Rotate option we called "Forming the Box," creates the overload situation on either side of the floor. Four men quickly form the box overload and many excellent shot possibilities are presented.

Allows for Good Outside Shooting

Against the 2-3 and 2-1-2 zone defenses, players are aligned in areas where there are no defensive men stationed. If one of the front two men covers the point man, then the wing guard will be open for the shot. Good outside shooting is necessary to pull the defense out and the 1-4 Blitz and Rotate patterns create the good shot possibilities.

Combines Inside-Outside Attack

In my opinion, the best method of attacking any defense is to combine both inside and outside attack possibilities. Each attack complements the other. For example, a good inside game forces the defense to sink or collapse toward the inside to cut off the high-percentage shots. The good outside shooter can force the defense to come back out to respect him, thus opening up the inside game again.

The 1-4 Blitz and Rotate Series uses these ideas of attacking a defense to the fullest. Previous percentages have shown that a balanced high-percentage attack is available and can be developed using this offense.

Adequate Continuity

Very little time should be wasted to reset an offense if a certain play does not work. The offensive series presented may be reset with only one pass and very little player movement. This continuity feature exists in most of the options presented throughout this book.

Good, Quick, High-Percentage Shots

Every offensive pattern used should produce a good high-percentage shot. This series was designed to produce just such shots in a short period of time with a minimum of ball handling. Our offensive goal is to score quickly and often and this offensive series creates the type of shots we prefer our players to take.

Difficulty for Match-Up Defenses

The 1-4 Blitz and Rotate Series is almost impossible for teams that try to use the match-up defenses. These teams must go man-to-man in order to match up and we believe the 1-4 attack with the rotating post men makes the defenses change quickly to either a man-to-man or a standard zone. If a coach disagrees, just apply the basic match-up rules to the play options described and see how confused your best defensive group will be after going through the 1-4 options.

1-4 BLITZ—ROTATE

The 1-4 Blitz and Rotation offense begins with the basic 1-2-2 alignment shown in Diagram 9-1.

Player 1 is the point man and should be the best ball handler and floor leader on the team. 1's offensive position is located at the top of the circle in direct line with the basket. Players 2 and 3 should be the best outside shooters and they set up on the imaginary line of the free-throw line extended. Players 4 and 5 are the post men. They set up in a low post position on each side of the free-throw lane.

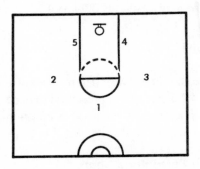

Diagram 9-1.

The series is predetermined by the coach or may be called orally by the point man, who calls "1-4 Blitz and Rotate" or just simply "1-4." As the call is made and the point man has moved the ball across the midcourt line, post men 4 and 5 cut to the high side post positions just outside the free-throw line (Diagram 9-2). This creates a one-man front with four men in a row on a line from sideline to sideline. This 1-4 alignment assures a good entry pass to one of the four men. If the pass is made to either 4 or 5 by 1, this keys the Blitz phase of the series.

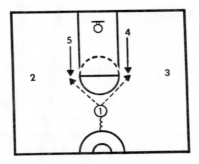

Diagram 9-2.

In Diagram 9-3, 1 passes to 4 at the high post position on the right side of the court. As soon as 4 receives the ball, 5 cuts across the middle to the basket. If 5 is covered, this usually opens up the high post area on the left side. 1 fills that position after 5 cuts and may receive a pass from 4.

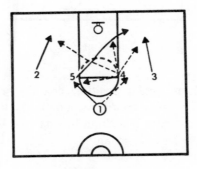

Diagram 9-3.

Wing guards 2 and 3 cut to baseline positions and face the man with the ball (4, in this case). The wing guards line up so they can shoot upon receiving a pass from 4 without having to dribble.

The options available for 4 are:

1. To shoot;
2. To pass to 5;
3. To pass to 1;

4. To pass to 2 on the left sideline; or

5. To pass to 3 on the right sideline.

If one of these options is not used, 1 steps out to get a return pass from 4 and resets the offense.

In Diagram 9-4, 1 passes to 4 at the high post position on the left side. As soon as 5 receives the ball, 4 cuts across the middle of the lane to the basket. If 4 is covered, this usually opens up the high post area on the right side. 1 fills that position after 4 cuts and may receive a pass from 5.

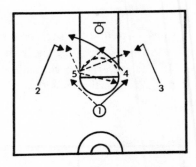

Diagram 9-4.

Wing guards 2 and 3 cut to positions near the baseline and face the man with the ball. The wing guards must be lined up so they can shoot upon receiving a pass from 5 without having to dribble.

The options available for 5 are:

1. To shoot;

2. To pass to 4, cutting down the middle;

3. To pass to 1 on the right side;

4. To pass to 2 on the left side; or

5. To pass to 3 on the right side.

If one of these options is not used, 1 steps out to get a return pass from 5 and resets the offense.

If the pass is made to either 2 or 3 by 1, this automatically keys the Rotate phase of the series (Diagram 9-5).

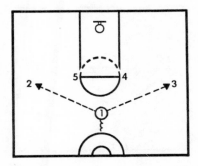

Diagram 9-5.

If 1 passes to 2, he immediately looks inside and may pass to 5 (Diagram 9-6). If this pass is not possible, 5 slides down the left side of the lane. 4 cuts across the lane. This maneuver creates a high-low alignment. 2 may pass to 4 who looks for a shot, for a possible pass to 5 in the low post area, or pass over to the right side to 3. If 2 passes to 5, he cuts to the corner where he may receive a return pass from 5. This is an excellent scoring option against the zone defenses.

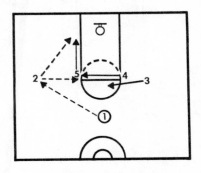

Diagram 9-6.

A variation called "Forming the Box" is keyed by 2 dribbling the ball to the left corner quickly after receiving a pass from 1 (Diagram 9-7). 5 slides down low. 4 cuts across the lane to the spot vacated by 5. 1 fills at the wing guard position formerly occupied by 2 prior to his dribbling to the left corner. 3 moves to the right high post position vacated by 4. 3 is also the defensive safety man if the ball is shot. He may also be the

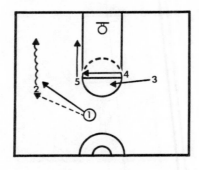

Diagram 9-7.

off-side rebounder, with 1 filling the defensive safety assignment.

Diagram 9-8 shows the options available if the ball is in the left corner. 2 may (1) shoot, (2) pass to 5, (3) pass to 4, or (4) pass to 1.

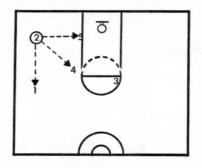

Diagram 9-8.

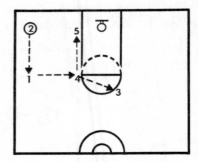

Diagram 9-9.

If the ball is passed back out to 1, he should look inside for 4 (Diagram 9-9). 4 should look for the other post man 5 because the zone will have begun shifting back to the right side. This option is a highly effective scoring option and illustrates our basic philosophy of taking the ball inside and to the basket at every opportunity. 4 may also pass across the free-throw lane to 3.

If 2 passes to 5, the first move by 5 is a power move on the inside. If 5 does not get a shot, 4 cuts to the basket for a possible pass from 5 (Diagram

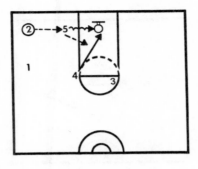

Diagram 9-10.

9-10). Coaches will be surprised at how many times this maneuver will produce a good power lay-up, even against much taller opponents.

The rotation option to the right side is shown in Diagram 9-11. 1 passes to 3 at the right wing guard position. 3 looks for a shot or may pass to 4 inside. If 4 does not receive a pass from 3, he slides down to a low post position and 5 cuts across the lane to the high post spot vacated by 4. 3 may pass to either post man.

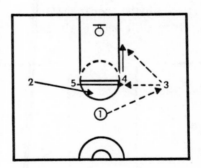

Diagram 9-11.

If the ball goes to 5 at the high post, he pivots to face the basket and may shoot or pass to 4 in the low post area. 3 should cut to the baseline toward the right corner after passing to 5. This cut often creates an open shot in the right corner.

In Diagram 9-12, 3, after receiving a pass from 1, drives quickly to

Diagram 9-12.

the baseline. Occasionally he will have a jump shot off the move. If not, we form the Box option on the right side. 4 slides down to the low post, 5 cuts over to form the high post corner, and 1 fills at the wing spot vacated by 3 driving to the corner.

Diagram 9-13 shows the options now open for 3 in the corner. He may (1) shoot, (2) pass to 4, (3) pass to 5, or (4) pass to 1. If the Box is formed quickly, most standard zones have difficulty covering all four of these spots. If 3 passes to 1, 1 may shoot or pass to 5 at the high post. 5 looks to 4 or to 3 and passes to the open man (Diagram 9-14). 1 may find 4 open as the zone starts to shift back to the left.

Diagram 9-13.

Diagram 9-14.

Diagram 9-15 shows the inside maneuver if 3 passes the ball to the low post man 4. 4 tries to use the power lay-up maneuver inside. Meanwhile, 5 cuts digonally across the lane and may receive a pass from

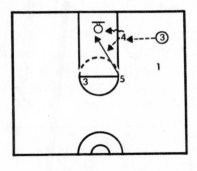

Diagram 9-15.

4. 4 may also pass back to 3 in the corner on the inside-out pass for a quick jump shot by 3.

If results are not produced by any of these moves, the ball is passed back to 1 to reset the offense. Once the players are accustomed to the pattern, good, high-percentage shots will result.

Varying Post Cuts

To counter the adjustment by the defense against the Blitz options, we added a variety of methods of sending the two post men to the two high post positions. The defensive men will have a more difficult time locating the two post men if they are cutting from different angles to the high post areas. Diagram 9-16 shows the "Y" post cut. The post cut may be called by the coach at a time-out or on a dead-ball situation. 4 and 5 cut across the lane to exchange positions with each other. Without stopping, both post

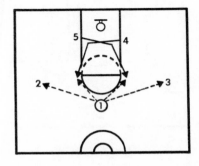

Diagram 9-16.

men cut to the two high post positions. 1 may pass to any of the four men on the entry pattern.

Diagram 9-17 illustrates the "X" cut. As 1 dribbles past the mid-court line, post men 4 and 5 cut across the lane to the high post positions opposite their original low post positions. 1 has the original four players to whom the entry pass may be made. The entry pass will key either the Blitz or the Rotate options.

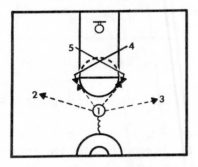

Diagram 9-17.

The third post cut option is the "L" cut (Diagram 9-18). As 1 dribbles across the mid-court line, post men 4 and 5 rotate to the two high post positions. 4 cuts straight up and then slides across to the left high post position. Meanwhile, 5 cuts across the lane and then up to the high post position on the right side. 1 has the four entry possibilities as previously diagrammed.

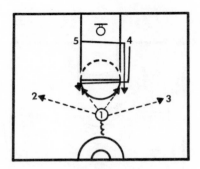

Diagram 9-18.

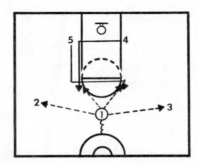

Diagram 9-19.

Diagram 9-19 illustrates the same "L" cut, but to the opposite side of the court. When 1 crosses the mid-court line, post men 4 and 5 begin the "L" cuts. 5 cuts to the left high post spot and on across to the right high post position. 4 cuts across the lane and on up to the left high post spot.

This cut establishes the original 1-4 entry offensive options. The second phase of the offense will be keyed by the entry pass from 1.

Wing Guards In

The latest addition to the series is the Wing Guards In entry. This option was included to add more variety to the offense and creates a different kind of defensive adjustment. This option is effective if the wing guards are capable of working inside and the post men can handle the ball outside.

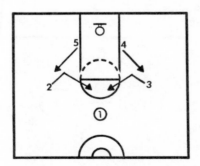

Diagram 9-20.

As 1 crosses the mid-court line with the ball, wing guards 2 and 3 cut into the two high post spots. Post men 4 and 5 replace the two wing guards (Diagram 9-20). This maneuver will give 1 the four original entry pass possibilities previously described in this chapter.

The advantages of this variation are:

1. The good ball-handling wing guards handle the ball, instead of the post men;
2. Interchanging positions makes the entry pass easier;
3. The variety opens up the entry passes on both the Wing Guards In option and the original 1-4 Blitz Rotate option; and
4. Creates additional movement.

The Wing Guards In option has opened up the ease with which the entry passes can be made.

1-3-1 Spot-Up Variation

The 1-3-1 Spot-Up Variation is included to show how we use the Spot-Up method of attacking certain standard zone defenses. This offense complements the 1-4 Blitz-Rotate options. The Spot-Up method refers to aligning players in the open areas of a zone defense and then moving the ball to the players located in the open areas quicker than the defense can slide to cover the ball.

The open areas on a 2-1-2 zone are shown in Diagram 9-21. The areas are circled and numbered to indicate where the players should set up to get the open shot.

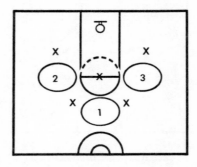

Diagram 9-21.

Diagram 9-22 shows the basic 1-2-2 alignment and the post cut to get into the 1-3-1 Spot-Up option. As 1 approaches the point position even with the basket, post man 5 cuts to the center of the free-throw line. This creates a 1-3-1 alignment. 1 may pass to 5, the first choice, or to either wing guard. 5 may shoot, if open, or pass to 4 who cut across the lane behind the zone as soon as 5 received the ball. 5 may also pass to wing guards 2 and 3. The wing guards are encouraged to shoot upon receiving a pass from 1.

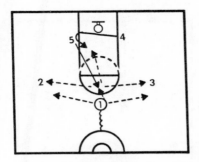

Diagram 9-22.

Diagram 9-23 shows the post rotation as the ball is passed from 1 to 3. Post man 5 cuts down the lane and may receive a pass from 3. If 3 passes back to 1, 4 cuts to the free-throw line. 1 may pass to 4 at the high post. 5 cuts behind the zone and may receive a pass from 4. If 4 shoots, 5 will be in the off-side offensive rebounding position. 4 may shoot or pass to either of the wing guards.

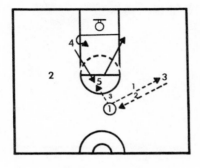

Diagram 9-23.

The wing guards always look inside and hit the post men at every opportunity. Both wing men should be good outside shooters so they can take advantage of shots from the open areas in the 2-3 or 2-1-2 zones.

Occasionally, against the 2-1-2 or the 2-3 zone defenses, we will use the Guard Penetration option shown in Diagram 9-24. The point man tries to split X 1 and X 2 and penetrate with the dribble to the free-throw line. This maneuver may be accomplished more easily after the point man receives a return pass from either one of the wing guards.

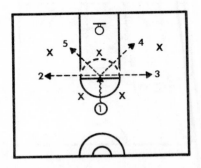

Diagram 9-24.

l may shoot, pass to one of the two low post men near the basket, or pass to either of the two wing guards.

The Guard Penetration option has been helpful in opening up the wing guards for excellent high-percentage jump shots. The defense must make some adjustments or be faced with giving up many close-in shots by l and 4 and 5 in the low post areas.

The 2-1-2 Spot-Up option is also a part of our offensive system, but will not be presented in this book.

CHAPTER **10**

Supplementing the 1-2-2
with an Auxiliary Offense

The auxiliary offense refers to any special play which a team uses to supplement the basic half-court offense. These special plays include out-of-bounds plays, jump-ball situations and controlled tempo or delay-game situations. With the adoption of the rule which allows an offended team to take the ball out of bounds on common fouls before reaching the bonus fouls, there are many more out-of-bounds situations in each game. Therefore, a team needs well-designed plays to cover these additional out-of-bounds situations.

A good out-of-bounds play should meet three requirements:

1. To get the ball into play safely;
2. To score if possible on the out-of-bounds situations; and
3. If a basket is not scored, to make the transition quickly into the regular half court offense.

The out-of-bounds plays presented in this chapter meet these requirements and have been thoroughly tested on the championship trail.

SIDELINE OUT-OF-BOUNDS PLAYS

"43" Out-of-Bounds Play

The alignment of personnel for "43" Out-of-Bounds play is as follows (Diagram 10-1): 1 is usually the point man. He is the team

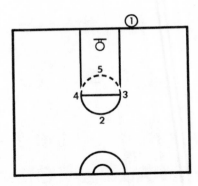

Diagram 10-1.

playmaker and has been taught how to read the defense and how to call the play designed to attack the defense being set by the opponents.

Several seasons ago, we ran into some unexpected problems while using the point man as the out-of-bounds ball handler. Our point man was only 5′ 6″ and he had trouble getting the ball in bounds when being covered by a much taller defensive guard. We used our tallest wing guard at the out-of-bounds spot and put the point man in the 2 spot. This solved the problem, and also, it helped us get into the team offense quickly if we did not score on the inbounds plays.

The 2 man's main assignments are to cut to the ball after the initial cut and to be the defensive safety man if the ball is turned over.

Wing guard 3 sets up at the high side post position on the ball side.

The 4 man is the quickest post man and he sets up at the left high post position opposite the ball. The biggest post man lines up in the 5 spot. He will be the Pick-and-Roll man on the play.

To key the play, 1 calls "43," prior to receiving the ball from the official underneath the basket. This point must be emphasized to the 1 man. By doing this, our four men have time to set up in the desired position without using any of the time allowed to put the ball into play.

1, after receiving the ball from the officials, slaps the ball to initiate the play. 5 moves to set a screen on 4. It is important to teach the 5 man to screen legally. If contact is made, the responsibility must be on the defensive man rather than 5.

4 must set up his cut by faking in one direction before cutting to the ball around the screen being set by 5. 5 will roll out to the basket after

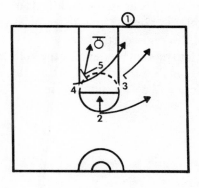

Diagram 10-2.

screening for 4. 5 should pivot on his right foot as he rolls to the basket (Diagram 10-2). 3 fakes left and cuts to the corner for a possible pass from 1.

The 2 man is the safety valve. He delays his cut until the other three players have made their cuts. If the first three options do not develop, 2 is instructed to get open to get a pass from 1. 2 must be alert to the situation and must not allow a five-second violation to occur because the ball has not been put into play.

Diagram 10-3 shows the ''43'' play as it looks being executed to the left side. On the left side, the 2 and 3 men change positions. This is done because 2 is in the area where he normally operates at the left wing guard position. 4 sets up on the opposite side of the lane away from the ball. 5 is

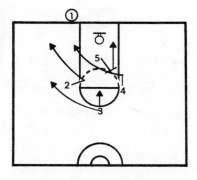

Diagram 10-3.

the primary screener and sets up in the middle of the lane in front of the basket facing the mid-court line. 3 lines up at the top of the circle in line with the basket and the mid-court circle.

1 puts the play into motion by slapping the ball. 5 screens for 4, who cuts to the basket around the screen. 5 rolls out to the basket. 2 cuts to the corner. 3 is the safety valve. 1's options are:

1. Pass to 4;
2. Pass to 5;
3. Pass to 2; or
4. Pass to 3.

After passing the ball in bounds, 1 cuts back out to the point position (if he is the point man) or to the wing guard position.

Another coaching point—teach 1 to be able to see all three cutters at once. This point will enable 1 to take advantage of all of the options that evolve from the play.

An optional variation may be executed by 4. If he is being overplayed to the ball and forced away from the direction of the original cut by the defense, 4 may fake into the lane and cut to the opposite side of the screen being set by 5. 5 reverse-pivots to the basket and rolls back to the right low post position (Diagram 10-4).

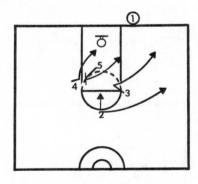

Diagram 10-4.

This is an effective variation that may be used without having to be called by the point man.

The "45" Out-of-Bounds Play

A special play was installed when our point man was extremely quick. This play was labeled "45." The same procedure is used by 1 as in the previously described out-of-bounds plays. 1 calls the play prior to accepting the ball from the official. 1 slaps the ball, 5 sets a stationary screen on 2's defensive man at the free-throw line. 2 sets his man up by step-faking in the opposite direction of his intended cut. 2 cuts to the basket around the screen set by 5. 5 will roll out after setting the screen (Diagram 10-5). Caution in rolling out should be taken to prevent the offensive block on the screen and roll.

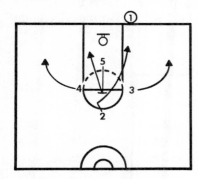

Diagram 10-5.

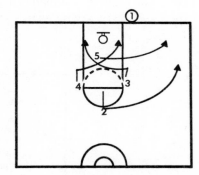

Diagram 10-6.

Wing men 3 and 4 flare-cut out toward the sidelines. These cuts are designed to keep the defense from sagging into the lane to help on the play.

If the defensive man on 5 switches to cover 2, a mismatch should be created with 5 being covered by a shorter defensive man.

The "46" Out-of-Bounds Play

The "46" play is a third variation incorporated into the auxiliary offensive system. 1 calls "46". He slaps the ball to set the play into motion. 5 sets a stationary screen in the middle of the free-throw lane. 3 cuts around the screen to the low post position on the left side. 4 fakes left and cuts off 5 to the right low post spot. 5 then cuts to the right corner. 2 is the safety valve if 1 has not passed to 3, 4 or 5 (Diagram 10-6).

Normally, the coach does not want the biggest post man in the corner, but we have found this to be an excellent safe method to get the ball in bounds.

The "44" Out-of-Bounds Play

The final baseline out-of-bounds play is the "44" play. Originally, this play was installed to use against zone defenses only, but we found it may be used very successfully against a man-to-man defense if the cutters will always set up each cut by a faking move in the direction opposite the intended cut.

All four players line up in single file along the side of the free-throw lane. The biggest post man is in the 5 spot, the second post man in the 4 spot, and the two wing guards line up in the 2 and 3 positions (Diagram 10-7).

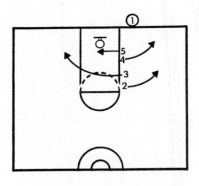

Diagram 10-7.

The basic rule that players 2, 3, and 4 follow is to cut in the direction opposite to the man in front of you.

1 calls the number "44" before taking the ball from the official. 1 slaps the ball. 5 fakes right and cuts to the left. 4 fakes left and cuts to the right corner. 3 fakes right and cuts into the lane. 2 fakes left and cuts to the right. 2 has a secondary responsibility because he is the man the longest distance from the ball. He is the safety valve and defensive man if a pass is not completed to 3, 4 or 5, or if a turnover occurs.

4 may key the direction of the cut by 5 by touching 5 on the side he wants him to cut. Varying the cut by 5 will tend to confuse the defense and make the in-bounds pass easier to complete.

Play 44 may be run against both the man-to-man and the various zone defenses.

SIDELINE OUT-OF-BOUNDS PLAYS

The "50" Play

The "50" Play is the first play in a three-play sideline out-of-bounds series. The alignment for "50" is shown in Diagram 10-8. Wing guards 2 and 3 set up in a straight line from the ball and the opposite sideline and about ten feet apart. The post men 4 and 5 set up in the normal post spots used in the regular offense. The point man 1 takes the ball out of bounds. 1 calls "50" prior to taking the ball from the official. To begin the play, 1 slaps the ball. 2 screens for 3 and rolls back to the ball after 3 cuts to the ball. 5 cuts to the corner. 4 cuts across the free-throw lane.

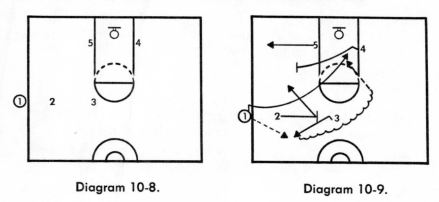

Diagram 10-8.   Diagram 10-9.

In Diagram 10-9, 1 passes to 3, who quickly dribbles back toward the basket. 4 sets a stationary screen for the out-of-bounds man 1. 1 fakes toward the man with the ball and then cuts hard around the screen by 4 to the basket. 3 may pass to 1 if he is open or set up the basic offense.

The "51" Play

The second play is called the "51" Play (Diagram 10-10). 1 calls "51" before taking the ball from the official. 1 then slaps the ball to put the play into motion. 5 fakes to the opposite direction and cuts hard toward the

Diagram 10-10.

ball. Wing guards 2 and 3 carry out the same pick-and-roll cut to get open. 1 passes to 5. As the pass is made, 4 cuts across the free-throw lane and sets a stationary screen about three strides past the lane. 1, after passing, walks in bounds for two or three steps, then cuts quickly around the screen by 4 to the basket. 5 hits 1 with the Alley Ooop pass if 1 is open. This is a good play to use late in the game when the defensive team is tired.

The play is set up by running play "50" a couple of times.

The "52" Play

This third play in the series is the "52" play. This play is effective against teams that try to play between the ball and their man. The alignment of the "52" play is shown in Diagram 10-11 with the cuts. 1 calls "52." The four players not involved in handling the ball out-of-

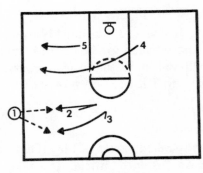

Diagram 10-11.

bounds line up in the same formation shown in plays "50" and "51." When 1 slaps the ball, all four men cut hard toward the sideline. Any player being overplayed reverses back in the opposite direction for a lob pass from 1. The initial cut sets up the reverse and also serves to clear out areas for the lob pass.

The same cuts may be used when facing zone defenses. The direct pass rather than the lob over may be used against the zone defenses.

The Sideline "44" Play

The final sideline play is called number "44." It is the same play as shown on Diagram 10-7, but is executed from the sideline.

1 calls "44" prior to receiving the ball from the official. Players 2, 3, 4 and 5 set up in a straight line between the man out of bounds and the opposite sideline (Diagram 10-12). The basic rule for 2, 3 and 4 is to cut in the opposite direction from the man in front of him. Player 5 keys the direction of the other players' cut. All players should fake in the direction opposite their intended cuts.

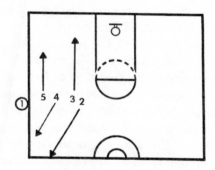

Diagram 10-12.

The "44" Play has been used as the only out-of-bounds play for the first few weeks of the season when the returning squad members are inexperienced and have a lot of new material to learn. As the players become more proficient, additional sideline and endline plays are added. It is better to learn one play well than to use the entire series without proper execution.

Out-of-bounds situations are stressed from the first day of practice and time is set aside in our daily practice plans. During the first four weeks of practice, we allot a minimum of ten minutes on the auxiliary offense phase of our season's preparation.

THE OFFENSIVE JUMP-BALL SERIES

The very first offensive plays that are taught on the first day of practice are the offensive jump-ball plays. The reason this play is taught first is that all games are started with the center jump. We feel there is a slight psychological advantage in getting the first jump ball of each quarter and if we can score on these recovered tips we are gaining control of the game from the beginning.

Our goal is to obtain the basketball and to score within four seconds. The offensive tip series presented in this chapter has been highly effective in our overall offensive system.

The basic alignment for the offensive center jump is shown in Diagram 10-13. The best jumper is stationed in the 5 spot. The quickest and best ball handler fills the 1 position. The best scoring wing guard is placed in the 2 spot with the second wing guard setting up in the 3 position. The number 4 position is filled by the post man not jumping.

5 tips the ball 1 who quickly drop-steps and drives to the basket. 2 cuts to the opposite side of the basket from 1 (Diagram 10-14). This creates a two-on-one situation if 1 pivots out quickly enough. If the play does not produce the good shot, the ball is passed back to 3 and the regular ball court offense is initiated. Players 4 and 5 move to their respective post positions while 3 cuts to the wing guard position behind 1.

If 3 receives the ball from 1, any of the basic post plays may be executed without having to pass the ball back to the pivot man.

If 5's defensive man lines up on the other side, 5 tips to the open side and the same movement as described in Diagram 10-14 occurs.

A variation is shown in Diagram 10-15. 5 signals to 1 to step back. 5 tips to 1 and the same offensive tip play is run. If the point man (1) lacks height, we will put the 4 man in the spot filled by 1.

This alignment is rather different from other traditional approaches, but we are sold on the results that have been produced. Of course, the coach must have a post man capable of getting a high percentage of jump balls.

During the first year we used the offensive tip formation, our team

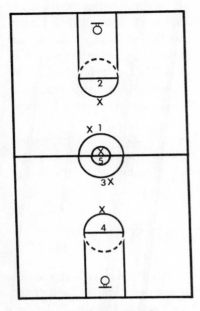

Diagram 10-13.

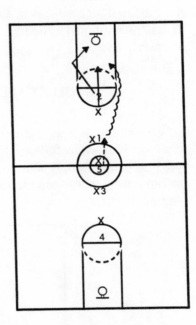

Diagram 10-14.

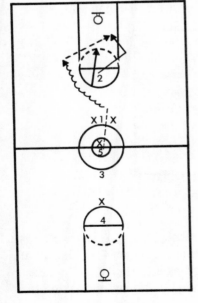

Diagram 10-15.

obtained 85 percent of the tips (92 of 108). The second season produced 96 of 112 tips for another 85 percent. Fortunately, we had a post man who was 6'6". As we discussed our plans for the third season, we found our starting post men were only 6'3" and 6'1", but were superior jumpers. We were reluctant to use the offensive tip because of the lack of height, but we experimented with the play in our spring workouts and during the summer league program. The results were still in our favor as we recovered almost 80 percent of the jump-ball situations.

Even in situations where we did not recover the tip, our opponents rarely scored because they had not been trying to score on the recovery. This unique offensive alignment has opened up a new dimension to our offensive system.

FULL-COURT PRESS OFFENSES

No offensive system is complete unless provisions have been made to attack the various full-court presses that are prevalent in basketball today. Three offensive attacks are shown to attack the various zone presses, plus one against the man-to-man presses.

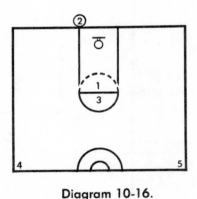

Diagram 10-16.

Diagram 10-16 shows the basic alignment. The quickest two players are set in a stack position at the free-throw line. Post men 4 and 5 set up at the mid-court line. The slowest wing guard takes the ball out of bounds. He must be a good passer and possess good judgment on making the inbounds pass.

The Pass and Go Away option is illustrated in Diagram 10-17. 2

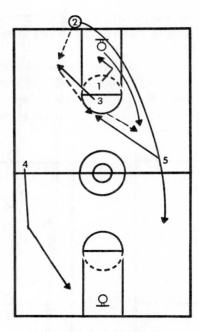

Diagram 10-17.

passes to 3 and cuts to the opposite side of the court. The post man opposite the ball cuts to the center area to get a pass from 3. 1 cuts up the sideline vacated by 5. 5 may pass to 1 or to 2 who trails the play. By flooding the area with two guards, we have found one of the men to always be open. 3 will stay behind the basketball at all times to be the safety valve.

The Pass and Hold option is shown in Diagram 10-18. The purpose

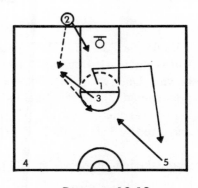

Diagram 10-18.

of this option is to form a diamond formation and then pass the ball quickly to the open man. 2 passes to 3 who quickly looks to the cutting post man from off side the ball.

Diagram 10-19 shows the diamond formation as the ball is moved up the court. Players are instructed to make short, quick passes. This pattern is used as a drill to get the players looking for the open man up the court. We put the ''no dribble'' rule in until the ball crosses the mid-court line to encourage the passing game.

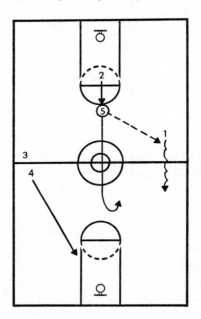
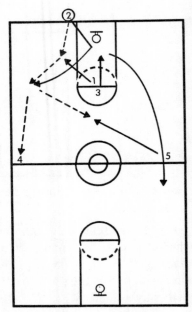

Diagram 10-19.   Diagram 10-20.

The third pattern used is the Pass and Hook option. The play begins with the same alignment as previously illustrated in this chapter. The Pass and Hook option is shown in Diagram 10-20. 2 passes to 1 and cuts down the middle. If 1 is double-teamed, 2 hooks back behind the trap for a return pass from 2. 5, the off-side post man, cuts to an open spot in the middle. 3 cuts into the open spot vacated by 5. 1 may pass to 5 or to 2, the hook-back man.

The player receiving the inbounds pass should pivot so that he can see the entire court. By doing this, the man with the ball can see the open man. Quick passing and player movement are essential to beating the zone presses.

The offensive pattern against the man-to-man type presses is very simple. All press offensive patterns are started from the same formation. Against man-to-man pressure, our philosophy is to get the ball inbounds safely to our 1 man and then clear out the area for him to operate one-on-one. If the ball goes to the 3 man, he is instructed to bring the ball down court in a one-on-one fashion. All other players are told to clear out, but keep their eyes on the man with the ball. If the ball handler is double teamed, the open player cuts to the ball or calls for the pass. This method of advancing the ball has proved highly successful and makes the double-teaming techniques by the defense virtually impossible.

TEMPO CONTROL—DELAY GAME

The final phase of the auxiliary offense is the tempo control offensive plays. For several years, we advocated a complete delay-type offense where we played for the foul only. This was exciting for the fans, but produced too many close games. We no longer shut down the offense completely.

Our tempo control offense is the Red Cat Shuffle described in detail in Chapter 5. The only change is that the players are instructed to shoot only unmolested lay-ups or very close-in jump shots. By shooting the high-percentage shots, the lead may be increased and additional pressure is applied to the defensive team to foul.

Another control tempo pattern is the Wheel Series explained in Chapter 7. This is a highly effective delay game. The same rules apply—take only the high-percentage lay-up or the very short jump shot.

Because the Red Cat Shuffle and the Wheel are similar offenses, we do not use both during the same season.

When running the delay game against the zone trap defenses, we sometimes use the Basic 1-2-2 offense described in Chapter 1, using the post rotation and the pass-and-go-away rule with the guards. Quick movement of the ball is emphasized.

Regardless of the type team a coach has, the tempo control offense will produce many beneficial results. We have used the tempo control style when we have key players in foul trouble in the second half, but need to keep them in the game. By not forcing the offense, we are able to run some time off the clock and still keep our key personnel in the game.

The Auxiliary Offense is a very important part of our total offensive system and should receive a permanent spot in the daily practice plans. One of the best ways we work on this phase of the game is the three-minute situation drill. Three minutes of time are placed on the clock. Our second team is given the ball out of bounds with a three-to-five-point lead. The first team must employ the necessary pressure defenses in order to get the ball and to score.

My assistant coach takes the second team and they will follow whatever strategy necessary to maintain their lead. These three-minute drills have been extremely valuable in providing the winning margins. Besides the strategy the players are learning, the three-minute situations provide competition and excitement to the practice sessions as well as being excellent conditioners. It is a good, positive way to end the daily practice session as well as getting the team prepared to handle the pressure of a tight ball game.

CHAPTER 11

Coaching Offensive Drills
for the 1-2-2

The purpose of this chapter is to illustrate some of the more important offensive drills used to teach various parts of the offense. No attempt will be made to describe the entire drill series we use, especially the equally important defensive drill series, because the theme of this book is offense.

Drills are an important part of the teaching process. We adhere to the whole-part method of teaching basketball. By the whole-part method, we mean that we show the complete offensive play, either on the blackboard or by distributing mimeograph copies of the material to be learned, and then break the complete play down into parts which become our offensive drills. By seeing the whole play and how the parts fit into the whole play, players will have a much better understanding of the drills being taught. This makes for quicker learning and produces more immediate results.

There are several precautions regarding drills that I feel each coach should consider.

First, many coaches use too many drills that are of no real value in teaching their specific offensive or defensive systems.

Second, many coaches drill too much. The bulk of our teaching on offense is down in the half-court phase of our daily practice plan. By teaching our offensive maneuvers in this manner, we get down to the one-on-one and two-on-two specifics as well as seeing the relationship between the maneuver being taught and the other men on the playing court.

The drills presented in this chapter are the ones we are currently using in the teaching of the 1-2-2 Offense.

POINT OF ENTRY DRILLS

The purpose of these drills is to be able to get the basketball to the place on the court from which the offense is to begin.

Get the Ball to the Spot Drill

The drill in Diagram 11-1 is designed to teach the offensive guards to get the ball to the head of the circle. One guard is given the ball and is closely pressured by a defensive man X 1. Considerable pressure and contact by the defensive man are allowed the first two weeks of practice. The offensive guard is taught to use the speed dribble, the crossover, the whirl, the stutter step, the stop-and-go dribble, as well as how to mix these dribble maneuvers to keep the defensive man off balance. The offensive man must get the ball to the taped "X" mark at the top of the free-throw circle.

The rotation in the drill is as follows: X 1 goes to the end of the guard line; the guard on offense becomes X 1; the next man in line becomes the offensive guard.

Stress the importance of being able to get the ball to the "X" mark.

Entry Pass Drill to the Wing Guards

Many of the offensive options described in this book depend on the point man getting the ball to the wing guards at the spot where we want the ball. Much emphasis in our pre-season practice is spent on teaching this principle. Drill 2, described in Diagram 11-2, is our key drill in teaching the wing guard entry pass.

At first, we will use only one wing guard at a time. Later, we add both offensive wing men. The purpose of this drill is to get the ball to the wing guards at a position no farther out on the court than an imaginary line drawn from sideline to sideline through the free-throw line. The wing guard must be taught to get open by using the "V" cut to the basket and back to meet the ball (Diagram 11-3), the "Z" cut (Diagram 11-4), the Reverse cut (Diagram 11-5), and the Hook cut (Diagram 11-6).

The wing guards are taught the four cuts plus how to walk their man down a few steps and cut quickly back to the ball. A defensive man is assigned to both 1 and 3 and told to deny the ball to 3.

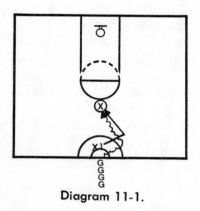

Diagram 11-1.

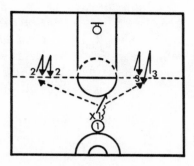

Diagram 11-2.

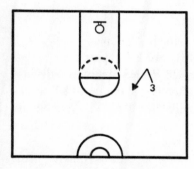

Diagram 11-3 (V Cut).

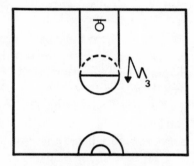

Diagram 11-4 (Z Cut).

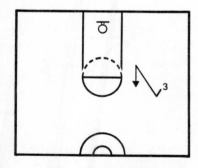

Diagram 11-5 (Reverse).

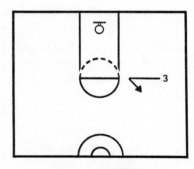

Diagram 11-6 (Hook).

3 must use every move to get open to get the ball inside the designated area. Taped lines are put on the floor as a guide to where we want 3 to receive the ball. Each player will stay in the 3 spot for at least five cuts before he rotates to the defensive position. The defensive man rotates to the end of the wing guard line.

Pressure is also applied to 1 to get the ball to the "X" before making his pass to 3.

Later, the 2 wing guard is added and 1 may pass to either 2 or 3.

This drill is down in our fundamentals-drill section of practice and the post men will be down at the other end of the court working on the post maneuvers.

This is a very important drill and all of the guards must possess the necessary skills to get open and in the spot where we want them for the entry pass.

Roll, Fan and Away Drill

To teach the three basic inside moves, the Roll, Fan and Away Drill is used. These maneuvers were described in detail in Chapter 1, so we will diagram them only to remind the coach which maneuvers we are discussing. Diagram 11-7 shows the "Roll-it" maneuver, Diagram 11-8 shows the "Fan-it" maneuver, Diagram 11-9 shows the "Away" maneuver, and Diagram 11-10 shows the "Wildcat Rotation" maneuver which may be used before calling any of the three basic post cuts.

At first, the maneuvers are done without using the defensive men. Then, we add two defensive post men and go through each of the three basic cuts. The post men try to score using the dribble, fakes and other offensive moves to get open.

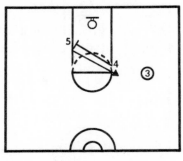

Diagram 11-7.

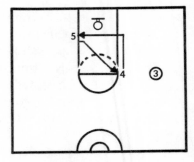

Diagram 11-8.

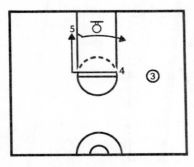

Diagram 11-9.

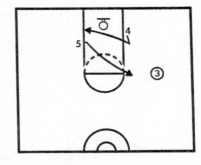

Diagram 11-10.

The coach working with the post men makes the pass. Later, we will use the wing guards. We also teach the post moves to the guards so they will be aware of the areas that will be open. This gives the guards a better understanding of when and where to pass the ball.

The rotation of the players is as follows: the offensive men go to the line on the baseline, the defensive men become offensive men, and the two new players become the defense. On a 15-man varsity squad we will keep six post men and nine guards. Included in the group will be the post men we expect to start during the season following the one we are presently in. This allows us to build for the future at all times.

Post Entry Drill

The Post Entry Drill was designed to (1) make the entry passes to either post man, (2) teach the wing guard reverse or back door cuts to the basket, and (3) teach the post special plays discussed in Chapter 6.

Step 1. Five offensive players are lined up in the basic 1-2-2 positions with defensive men covering post men 4 and 5.

Step 2. 1, the point man, will call "Post" and the two post men will fake and cut to the high side post positions on each side of the free-throw lane looking for a pass from 1.

Step 3. After 1 passes, the wing guard on the ball side reverse-cuts to the basket as fast as he can go and 1 cuts around the post man with the ball. The post man may hit the cutting wing man, 1, or wait for the wing guard cutback.

Step 4. The 1 man, after cutting around the post man with the ball and not receiving a return pass, continues on down and sets a screen on the

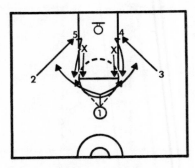

Diagram 11-11.

wing guard who had reversed to the basket and now cuts back behind 1's screen for a possible pass from the post man.

Three additional defensive men are added to make the drill a five-on-five drill. This is an excellent drill that incorporates three different plays into one drill.

TEACHING THE PICK AND ROLL

One of the popular offensive options in this area of the country is the Pick and Roll (Screen and Roll) Option. This option is usually a two-man offensive play between a guard (point or wing guard) and a big post man. One of the objectives of the play is to create a switch situation with the defensive post man switching to cover the offensive guard and the defensive guard switching on the bigger offensive center. This allows the offensive guard to pass the ball inside to the Rollout Man (offensive center) for the close-in shot while being covered defensively by a smaller guard.

There are four ways we incorporate the Pick and Roll options into our offense. These methods are illustrated in Diagrams 11-12, 11-13, 11-14 and 11-15.

Diagram 11-12 shows the Pick or Screen by the post man for 1. This option occurs when using the regular clear option on the Clearout series. The object is to brush 1's defensive man off on 5's screen, create a switch with the opponent's center covering the 1 man, rolling the post man 4 to the basket where he may receive a pass from 1 for the inside offensive maneuver—hopefully a power lay-up.

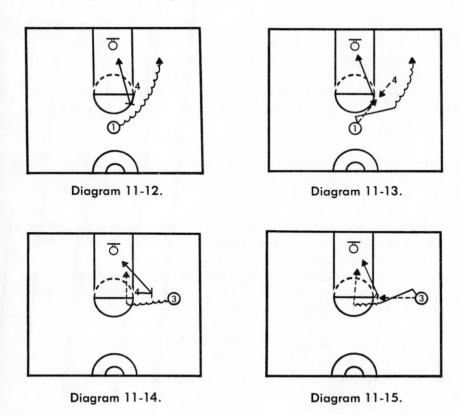

Diagram 11-12.

Diagram 11-13.

Diagram 11-14.

Diagram 11-15.

The key coaching hints are:

1. The post man must set a legal stationary screen;
2. The point man must set up the defensive man by faking a drive to the opposite side before dribbling around the post screen;
3. The Rollout man must pivot so he can see the ball at all times; and
4. The Rollout man should be aware of off-side help by the defense to avoid the offensive charge on the play.

Diagram 11-13 shows the same play except 1 passes to 4, fakes left, and cuts around 4 to get the ball back. 4 rolls out to the basket after returning the ball to 1.

Diagram 11-14 shows the Pick and Roll play being executed from the 3 wing guard position. 3 dribbles past a stationary screen being set by 4. 4 rolls out to the basket after screening. 3 may shoot at any time as he drives off the screen.

Diagram 11-15 is the Pick and Roll play with the pass from 3 to the post man 4. After passing, 3 fakes right and "V"-cuts around 4 for a return pass. 4 rolls out to the basket.

This is the same play as the "Name" option described in Chapter 1. 3 may fake left and reverse-cut to the basket (Give and Go) if being heavily pressured by the defense.

All four methods are taught on both sides of the court. After the players become acquainted with each method of developing the Pick and Roll option, defensive men are added to the drill. These drills provide many key offensive and defensive situations with which the players must cope in a game situation.

The final step in the drill is to go five-on-five and use the same play series. This gives the players the complete picture of where all of the other players are located in relation to the ball.

Coach Ray Mears at The University of Tennessee popularized the post screen options in this area. However, he did not use his big man on the roll-out because of the offensive charging possibility. Our adjustment cut on the roll-out was previously described in Chapter 1 and the coach may want to consider the roll-out and the advantages it presents for the high-percentage basket.

THE SHUFFLE CUT DRILLS

There are four types of Shuffle cuts utilized in our offensive system. These four cuts are shown in Diagrams 11-16, 11-17, 11-18 and 11-19.

Diagram 11-16 illustrates the Back Door Shuffle Cut discussed in Chapter 5 (the Red Cat Shuffle) and Chapter 7 (the Wheel Series from the 1-2-2). This can be a very productive option if the cutter can set up his cut effectively.

The ball is in the right wing guard position. The coach or one of the wing guards can pass the ball. I prefer the wing guards handling the ball so I can be free to teach and correct the movements of the drill.

5 moves out to set a stationary screen on 2's defensive man. 2 must set up the screen by faking a cut into the lane or by walking his man down

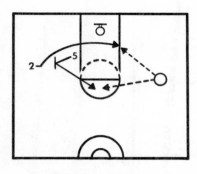 

Diagram 11-16   **Diagram 11-17.**

into a position where the screener can block the defensive man when 2 cuts along the baseline. 5 will screen and roll back to the left high post position (Red Cat Shuffle Option).

Diagram 11-17 shows the first cut on the Wheel Series. 5 sets a stationary screen for 2 slightly farther out than in Diagram 11-17. 2 fakes toward the baseline and cuts over the top of 5's screen to the basket to receive a pass from the man with the ball.

Diagram 11-18 shows the Baseline Shuffle Cut off the Exchange and Clearout Series. Both post men form a double screen for 2, the off-side wing man. 2 sets his man up by walking him down behind the screen area and cuts along the baseline.

Later, the 4-5 Swing Option is added because defensive players will tend to play the offensive play. The Swing option was installed as a counter move to prevent the defensive overplay.

Diagram 11-18.

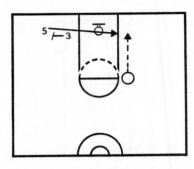

Diagram 11-19.

Diagram 11-19 shows the Baseline cut off the Red Cat Shuffle. This is a second phase of drill 11-16. The wing guard 3 would become the screener for the post man.

All of these drills are key parts of the offensive series described, and proper execution is essential for success. The same options are run when we get into the five-on-five half-court offensive development section of practice.

DEVELOPMENT OF SUCCESSFUL STACK CUTS

Two very important phases of the 1-2-2 offense are the Stack cuts and the off-side Swing options which are variations of the Stack cuts. Exact timing is essential if these options are to produce desirable results.

There are three sets of Stack options that should be covered. These are shown in Diagrams 11-20, 11-21 and 11-22.

Step 1. The 2-5 Stack cut is taught first. Wing guard 2 establishes a position behind 5 on the baseline side. 2 and 5 face the ball (at 1 spot). As the point man approaches the top of the free-throw circle, 2 fakes into the lane, cuts back around 5 for a possible pass from 1 (Diagram 11-23).

Step 2. 2 may shoot if he is open, drive to the middle, or to the outside or pass to 5 on the inside. 5 is instructed to roll out to the basket if 2 drives into the free-throw lane area. He may receive a pass or be in excellent offensive rebounding position if the shot is taken by 2.

Diagram 11-20 shows the 3-4 combination. This drill is executed the same as the 2.5 combination, except on the other side of the free-

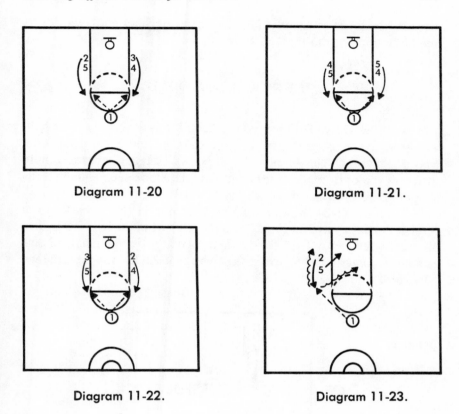

Diagram 11-20

Diagram 11-21.

Diagram 11-22.

Diagram 11-23.

throw lane. The Stack cut may be used to free the wing guards for an entry pass in addition to being a scoring play.

Diagram 11-21 shows the Post Stack combination that may be used. Apply the same rules as described above.

Diagram 11-22 illustrates the Stack combinations when the opposite wing guards cut on the Scramble call. This maneuver is used to get certain combinations of players together to create a defensive mismatch. For example, if the defensive man covering 2 is much shorter, we may want the 2 man and the 4 man working together to create a defensive mismatch inside for 4. The point man would call "Scramble Across" and then run the Stack play with 2 and 4 on the right side.

The use of the various combinations of Stack options enables the offense to create favorable high-percentage shots and requires the defensive team to adjust constantly. For this reason the Stack and Swing drills should be included in the 1-2-2 offense.

THE PICK DOWN DRILL

The Pick Down Drill is used to teach players to screen off the ball. This maneuver is used extensively in the Red Cat Shuffle Series and in the Special Plays—Double Option. These picks or screens occur at slightly different angles from the Shuffle cuts and the Stack cuts, and the drills should be added to teach these cuts.

Diagram 11-24 shows the Pick Down option (from the Red Cat Shuffle). 5 passes to 3 and cuts down the left side of the free-throw lane and sets a screen on 4's defensive man. 4 fakes into the lane and cuts around the screen set by 5. 3 passes to 4 who looks for the jump shot or for a pass to 5.

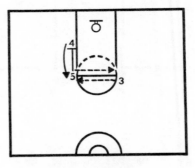

Diagram 11-24.

If a switch occurs, 5 is instructed to step in to the lane for a possible pass from 3. This Step-In option is also a part of the Double Left and Double Right options described in Chapter 6. A basket off the Step-In option can be demoralizing to the opposition because of the spectacular effect of the play.

The same option to the right side is shown in Diagram 11-15. 2 passes to 5 and cuts down the right side of the free-throw lane and sets a stationary screen for 3. 3 fakes into the lane and cuts behind 2's screen to the right high post. 5 may pass to 3 or to 2 on the Step-In option.

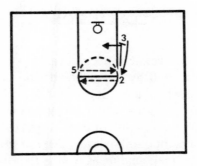

Diagram 11-25.

The Double Left Drill is shown in Diagram 11-26. 1 passes to 3 and sets a screen for the opposite wing guard. 5 also screens for 2. 2 fakes a baseline cut, then cuts back to the free-throw line for a pass from 3. 3 may hit 1 on the Step-In option if an improper switch occurs between 2 and 1's defensive men. The regular play may be used as a drill by adding 4 to the play.

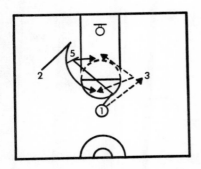

Diagram 11-26.

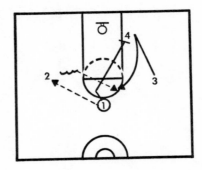

Diagram 11-27.

Diagram 11-27 illustrates the Double Right Drill. 1 passes to 2 and sets a double screen with 4 for the wing guard on the right side 3. 3 fakes a baseline cut and cuts back to the free-throw line for a possible pass from 2. 2 may pass to 1 on the Step-In option if an improper switch occurs.

These drills are very helpful in teaching the basic options of the 1-2-2 offense presented throughout this book.

CONCLUSION

This book has put together an accumulation of tested 1-2-2 offensive plays that have been used by the author during the past 13 years of coaching on the high school level. It is hoped that a few ideas have been presented that the reader has not tried, and that they will be adopted and be helpful in improving the coach's offensive system.

I would like to point out, however, that our program also stresses aggressive defense and rebounding as well as thorough coverage of the individual fundamentals. No offensive system will produce championship teams unless all phases of the game are developed. So, teach the fundamentals first, then the offensive execution will become more effective. *The 1-2-2 Offense for Winning Basketball* will then be useful in developing a winning program.

INDEX

INDEX